IRELAND

of one hundred years ago

The interior of St Patrick's Anglican Cathedral, Dublin. Although the second (after the tenth-century Christ Church), it was recognised as the 'National' Cathedral of the Church of Ireland, first having been raised to cathedral status in the thirteenth century. Here Jonathan Swift was Dean, from 1713–45. Although disestablished by Act of Parliament in 1869, the Church of Ireland retained its 'establishment' role at the top of the social pyramid.

Belleek Pottery, Belleek, Co Fermanagh, showing the moulding room. The pottery was famed for its distinctive interlaced patterns and the lustre of its finish.

IRELAND

of one hundred years ago

D A V I D   H A R K N E S S

S U T T O N   P U B L I S H I N G

First published in 1999 by
Sutton Publishing Limited · Phoenix Mill
Thrupp · Stroud · Gloucestershire · GL5 2BU

Copyright © in this compilation David Harkness, 1999

British Library Cataloguing in Publication Data
A catalogue record for this book is available from the British Library

ISBN 0-7509-1728-8

Photo, p. i: the Ogham Stone at Aghascrebagh, near Cookstown, Co Tyrone, displays an example of early Irish writing. Originally with twenty letters, later twenty-five, the alphabet was composed of varying slashes incised on the edge of a stone (or piece of wood), dating generally from the fourth to the seventh centuries; p. iii: South Main Street and Clockgate (which once served as a gaol), Youghal, Co Cork, *c.* 1900. A barracks town, its population in 1901 was 5,393; p. 1: Portadown foundry workers celebrate the relief of Ladysmith, 7 February 1900.

 ALAN SUTTON™ and SUTTON™ are the trade marks of Sutton Publishing Limited

Typeset in 11/13pt Bembo Mono.
Typesetting and origination by Sutton Publishing Limited.
Printed in Great Britain by
WBC Limited, Bridgend.

A group in front of Mathew McSwiggin's public house, an appropriately named north-west Ulster version of a popular feature of both urban and rural life.

CONTENTS

Introduction vii

1 Guidebook Ireland 3

2 Governance 20

3 Earning a Living 38

4 Recovering the Past .56

5 Sport, Entertainment and Leisure 71

6 Mind and Body: Education, Health and Housing . . .88

7 Soul: Religion in Ireland 107

Photographic Credits & Text Sources 119

Index 120

The coaster Davaar *aground on the rocks at Groomsport, Co Down, 7 June 1895.*

Noblesse Oblige: Mrs Cavendish Butler visits with Mrs Britten, Tempo village, Co Fermanagh, 12 July 1900.

The launch party before the naming ceremony of the Walmer Castle (342) on 6 July 1901. W.J. Pirrie, at that time the leading figure in Harland and Wolff, is third from the right, and standing next to him is Sir Donald Currie, Chairman, Union Castle Line. G.W. Wolff, founder, is fifth from the left in the white hat. (See also pp. 53 and 54.)

Women workers at Lambkin's tobacco factory, Fishers Street, Merchants Quay, Cork, in the early part of the twentieth century.

INTRODUCTION

There is no doubt that, as the nineteenth century gave way to the twentieth, Ireland was experiencing remarkable change. In politics there were those determined to cling to the status quo, the existing unitary United Kingdom, governed from Westminster with an additional Irish administration centred on Dublin Castle. However, an even greater number was demanding devolution of power to an Irish Parliament, a Home Rule Parliament dealing with Irish affairs though still within the existing state and still part of the British Empire. An indefinable section wished to go further and to break completely from Britain and form an independent Irish republic.

At the centre of power, the competing Conservatives and Liberals had parted company on this central issue in 1886, Liberals judging that the preservation of the Union was best served by a measure of Irish management of Irish affairs, the Conservative and Unionist Party adamant that devolution would lead to separation and that the answer to Irish discontent was the removal of grievances and the creation of a national harmony that would embrace both islands. The traditional landed classes and the representatives of the industrial north, the largely Protestant 25 per cent of the population, stood for the status quo. The Catholic majority, increasingly enfranchised by parliamentary reform and local government changes, notably the Third Reform Act of 1884 and the Irish Local Government Act of 1898, looked for devolution or more, the bulk of them supporting their own Home Rule Party, created in 1870. And it should be noted that the proper structure of local government, that is urban and rural district councils and county and borough councils introduced in 1898, had begun to provide a useful training ground, especially for the advocates of autonomy.

Social trends had already ensured that the power of the landed elite was in decline and that a new bourgeoisie was appearing with political and economic ambitions. Loss of landed parliamentary dominance was mirrored by landed economic loss as agitation and legislation combined to reduce rents and lessen the attractions of life on landed estates. Wealth was beginning to transfer to a rising middle class, but alterations in economic standing themselves produced a battleground in rural Ireland, as the small farmers, increasingly owners rather than tenants (and here the greatest advance was to occur with the Land Act of 1903), sought to free themselves from the grip of traditional suppliers of goods and credit and by co-operation to improve the production and sale of their produce to their own benefit. In this contest Horace Plunkett, Protestant and Unionist though he was, stands out as the pioneer of rural reorganization and self-help.

Technical advance allied to government investment had brought road and rail to remote parts, opened up markets and facilitated tourism on a scale amplified by increases in disposable income and leisure time. The pace of life was beginning to increase, unrelated advances were cumulatively bringing unanticipated and to a degree unmanageable results. Yet all the while, Irish people continued to leak away from the country, to Britain and beyond, the census returns of 1891, 1901, and 1911 telling their own story: population was recorded at 4,704,750, 4,458,775 and 4,390,219 respectively.

Ireland was at the dawn of a new era, at a cross-roads, at a moment when significant choices beckoned. It was in flux and as such it is now difficult to capture accurately the condition of its land and people at that time. But we can try, with Queen Victoria, to do so. Long reluctant to visit Ireland or to recognize the worth of her Irish subjects, she was moved by the valour of the Irish regiments in South Africa to visit Dublin in 1900. She was too advanced in years to travel beyond her Irish capital, but a photographic display of the work of the Congested Districts Board, a government initiative of the early 'nineties, which was mounted for her, must have convinced her of Ireland's regional variety: East to West as good land gave way to bad and proximity to markets yielded to distance; North to South, that is from a colder, more Protestant and industrial North to a warmer, Catholic and largely rural South. She stayed at the home of her representative, the Lord Lieutenant, and met her officials and the leading members of Irish society. Gratifyingly, her subjects turned out to give her a friendly welcome, despite the discouragement of their more advanced political leaders.

Victoria would have gained, too, some impression of the renewal of interest in Ireland's past and in those traditions and special features that evidenced Ireland's uniqueness and difference from the larger island (the 'mainland' as Britain was wont to be called). In Ireland, the reawakened interest in ancient sites and artistic achievements was given focus by a revival of the Irish language and the folk literature and sagas that it enshrined, and this in turn inspired an upsurge in poetry, drama and literature drawing on ancient sources, but in the English language, a movement of universal quality but one destined to clash with the particularism of Irish nationalism and to cause argument and dissension in the first decade of the new century.

How Ireland was governed, how Irishmen earned their livelihood, how Ireland's cultural heritage was revived are all part of the spectrum that was Ireland in this era of change and these elements are reflected in the chapters that follow. So too is the world of leisure. The world of sport, for example, was

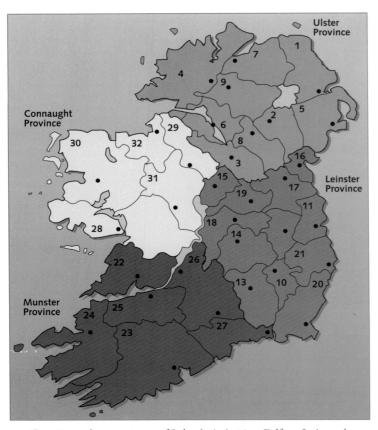

*Counties and county towns of Ireland: 1 Antrim: Belfast; 2 Armagh:
Armagh; 3 Cavan: Cavan; 4 Donegal: Lifford; 5 Down: Downpatrick;
6 Fermanagh: Enniskillen; 7 Londonderry: Derry; 8 Monaghan:
Monaghan; 9 Tyrone: Omagh; 10 Carlow: Carlow; 11 Dublin: Dublin;
12 Kildare: Naas; 13 Kilkenny: Kilkenny; 14 Queen's: Maryborough;
15 Longford: Longford; 16 Louth: Dundalk; 17 Meath: Navan;
18 King's: Tullamore; 19 Westmeath: Mullingar; 20 Wexford: Wexford;
21 Wicklow: Wicklow; 22 Clare: Ennis; 23 Cork: Cork; 24 Kerry:
Tralee; 25 Limerick: Limerick; 26 Tipperary: north – Nenagh, south –
Clonmel; 27 Waterford: Waterford; 28 Galway: Galway; 29 Leitrim:
Carrick-on-Shannon; 30 Mayo: Castlebar; 31 Roscommon: Roscommon;
32 Sligo: Sligo.*

thanks to pioneering national provision from the 1830s onwards, was generally thought to be backward and inadequate at secondary level (or 'intermediate' as it was known). Technical education was in its infancy, while at university level provision was small and controversial. Dublin University had served Protestants since 1592, and three non-denominational colleges had been founded in Cork, Galway and Belfast in 1845. A small Catholic college, established in Dublin in 1854, had not met the demand for a state-funded Catholic university and an acceptable compromise was not to be reached until 1908 with the establishment of the National University of Ireland. This embraced the University Colleges in Cork, Galway and now Dublin but recognized the different nature of the North-east by turning Queen's College Belfast into a separate university.

Like education, health provision also reflected past government rather than private initiative with an extensive if fairly primitive structure of local dispensaries, county fever hospitals and asylums, and some specialist public hospitals in the major centres. Basic facilities were also present in many of the workhouses, spread over 130 poor law districts, and some of these were to form the nucleus of local cottage hospitals in the future. Housing, dire in mid-century, had been somewhat improved since the Famine. The Big Houses still stood, while the smallest cabins were being replaced. In between, the trend was towards better standards of construction and comfort.

Religion remained a prominent feature of Irish life, and there had been a resurgence in church building in Catholic parishes throughout the nineteenth century, with an added enthusiasm for Roman conformity and discipline from the mid-century onwards, rather than the traditionally more relaxed Irish practices. The Protestant denominations had experienced their own renewals of faith and practice in the second half of the century and their rivalries and their minority position in a predominantly Catholic country kept religion to the fore and both church attendance and theological argument vigorous, with regrettable outbursts of sectarianism and bigotry from time to time.

Naturally, all these characteristics were further coloured by national and international events: the celebration of the centenary of Ireland's 1798 Rising provoking much contemporary speculation; the Boer war drawing republican volunteers to the support of the Afrikaaners as well as Irish regiments to uphold the authority of the Crown; Royal jubilees and visits, not to mention the death of Victoria and accession of Edward, occasioning political argument; Trade Union activity clashing with traditional bosses; women demanding educational equality and, more tentatively, the suffrage. Such things, with periodic strikes, riots and cattle driving excursions form the background to the chapters ahead.

But the past has rightly been likened already in this series of volumes to a 'foreign country', and it is with the eye of a tourist, therefore, and in the company of contemporaries, lured by the new railways and their steamship associates, with their new hotels and comprehensive guidebooks, that the reader is invited to begin this journey to 'Ireland of 100 years ago'. Bon voyage.

David Harkness

now increasingly available and increasingly formalized, as rules and leagues and fixtures began to reflect the shortening of the working week, the freeing up of Saturday afternoons, and the increase in communications by bus and rail that made home and away matches possible for players and followers alike. Bicycles, motor-cycles and cars, available for leisure and enjoyment of the countryside as well as facilitating movement, were soon harnessed to the competitive sporting calendar, with races, trials and gymkhanas joining those activities already familiar to athletes, horse lovers and the whole range of team sportsmen and women, both 'native' and 'garrison', while many individual games, from croquet to tennis, continued to flourish. The world of entertainment also expanded. Music hall and theatre and the new cinema were more accessible, while dancing and ploughing matches, flower shows, and 'bring and buy' sales, fêtes and whist drives contributed as before to an astonishing range of pastimes, which can only be glimpsed at in the pages ahead.

Irish education, although well regarded at primary level

IRELAND

of one hundred years ago

Carlingford, most northerly town of the medieval 'Pale', situated on the sea lough that divides Louth from Down. Note the thirteenth-century Kings John's Castle by the harbour and the Mourne Mountains 'sweeping down to the sea' in the background. Today the lough forms the eastern end of the border between Northern Ireland and the Irish Republic.

General view of the Upper Lake, Killarney, Co Cork, one of the most popular tourist destinations in this era of burgeoning tourism.

Chapter 1

GUIDEBOOK IRELAND

*T*he 1906 edition of Black's Guide to Ireland, *while noting the across-the-board improvement of hotel accommodation in Ireland, felt there was still need for further progress, especially at the more modest end of the market. Although enthusiastic about developments in travel – Ireland's cheap and swift steamship services and internal railway systems were then offering 'the English holiday-maker of slender means the most attractive facilities for travelling in Western Europe' – at the same time it warned that Irish time was 25 minutes later than Greenwich, and that the Irish mile was longer than its English counterpart: 11 of the former being equal to 14 of the latter. The Guide then proceeded to describe the opportunities for cycling on Ireland's roads, the joys of the Irish scenery, and the traditional lure of fishing (but avoid August) before pursuing a more conventional resumé of the cultural, historical and geological features of this desirable destination. It is a pattern followed by other guides, notably those issued by the steamship and railway companies. By 1911, the task of being 'just to the (hotel) landlord, and at the same time faithful to the traveller' remained, according to the* Thorough Guide Series *on Ireland, a delicate one,*

but by now not only fishing was highlighted (the established How and where to fish in Ireland *by Hi-Regan being recommended) but also golf, the many new courses (most still but 9 holes) being tabulated. Ireland, with its Tourist Association active, was firmly on the map for that new and rising section of the British population with annual holidays, disposable income and access to inexpensive travel.*

Transport too was experiencing rapid change. The ubiquitous 'side' or 'jaunting' car was experiencing competition from charabanc and motor car, although the presence of horseshoe nails on the surface of the roads was a problem for the recently introduced pneumatic tyres. Railways, though, were the greatest source of mobility and by the year 1900 had reached almost their fullest extent, with a widespread standard network supplemented by a light railway system in the North and South-west. The romance of steam was undimmed, as yet unchallenged by motor bus and lorry that were so soon to render rail uneconomical.

Here, as in so much that follows in this book, we can observe the impact of momentous change wrought by nineteenth-century energy and invention. One hundred years ago an extraordinarily exciting age was dawning, not least for the traveller and holiday-maker.

Ballynahinch Lake and Castle, Co Galway, a part of what was at one time the largest estate in the British Isles. It had belonged to the Martin family, of which Violet Martin, collaborator of Edith Somerville, was a member. Thomas Martin had bankrupted himself feeding the poor during the famine years and the Castle then passed to others, including the famous cricketer Ranjit Sinhji, in the 1920s.

The Three Jolly Pigeons, a hostelry near Auburn, Co Westmeath, the village from which
Oliver Goldsmith drew his inspiration for The Deserted Village.

PANORAMAS AND PATRIOTS

There, on 'John Bull's Other Island' are to be found attractions incomparable, and problems innumerable – topographical and scenic, archaeological, sociological, industrial, political, religious. In that little country, smaller than the State of Maine, are to be found the largest lake, the greatest river, and, with one exception, the loftiest mountain in the Kingdom. Irish products are famed the world over – the marble of Connemarra, the china of Belleek, the crochet of Cork, the lace and bacon of Limerick, the linen of Belfast, the poplins and tweeds of Dublin and other centers. There are the ship yards, the tobacco factories, and the breweries among the largest in all the world. There are great cathedrals, great universities, great libraries, and great museums. There are great mansions in delightful demesnes. There are picturesque ruins of castles, monasteries, abbeys, towers and walls. In old cairns, cromlechs, mounds and monuments are to be recognized traces of a prehistoric age, ever exciting new

wonder as they are the more thoroughly explored. The whole Island is fringed with a panoramic succession of rugged headlands and rounded hills, bewitching bays, estuaries and glens, while fertile fields offer up their incense of rich increase to the Most High.

More interesting than Ireland is the Irishman himself. He is not to be imagined a despairing pauper, nor, on the other hand, a flippant purveyor of haphazard humour. He may be poor, and sometimes witty, but at heart the real Irishman is a philosopher and a patriot. Humour is the soul of his philosophy, hope the life of his patriotism. In some sections, filth, wretchedness, disease and poverty are still alarmingly in evidence, but the pig-in-the-parlor, the shillalah, and the inverted pipe are not conspicuous features in modern life. Old types remain, but a new order prevails. There is much to learn and to unlearn, much to see and to enjoy, to admire and to deplore in a tour around the Emerald Isle.

William Charles O'Donnell

Kingstown Harbour. Dun Leary (Dun Laoghaire to-day) was renamed Kingstown in 1821 to honour its use by the departing King George IV. It was soon the main port of entrance from Britain (via Holyhead).

GEORGE AND THE OBELISK

The first object that meets the eye on landing is a squat and ugly obelisk, surmounted by a crown lying on a cushion. The emblem is not badly chosen to remind one of the idle and voluptuous monarch, in memory of whose visit to Ireland in 1821 this monument was erected. The name of 'Kingstown' was then given to this little harbour instead of 'Dunleary', which signifies 'Fort of Leary', one of the last Celtic Pagan Princes. One would naturally imagine this was the place where George IV landed when honouring his Irish subjects. Not at all; it is where he re-embarked on his departure. Was it for him or for them that the remembrance of this glad day was immortalized in granite?

Madame de Bovet

STEAK FOR BREAKFAST?

There are some excellent hotels in Ireland. Dublin, Belfast, and all the more prominent tourist resorts are provided with hostelries containing all modern conveniences and comforts. But in the Irish country-town hotel there are few modern conveniences. Bath rooms are few and primitive beyond belief. Many of the smaller hotels are lighted with oil lamps or even with the old-fashioned tallow candles. One finds it difficult to have a fire kindled in one's room, though it is often as cold and damp in Ireland in midsummer as it is in our country in April and November.

And naturally the service is slow. When the young lady clerk sends the porter to your room for information as to what you wish for breakfast, you send word back that you would like to have a steak, some Irish bacon, potatoes, scrambled eggs on toast, and cocoa. Then you wash, shave yourself (for there are few barbers in Ireland), dress in a leisurely manner, find your way down through labyrinthian windings to the street level, take a walk about town, make some purchases of souvenirs, talk with country peasants upon the street corners, come back to the hotel office, write a letter or two, send off a batch of souvenir post-cards, then repair to the dining-room and open the morning newspaper and begin to search therein for news. Continue this search long enough and the good-natured waiter will break into your labors with as good a breakfast as any one could wish. The Irish pride themselves upon their mutton, beef, and butter. And all kinds of fowl may be had for a pittance. There will be no pies upon the table, for the Irish people do not care greatly for 'sweets', but no breakfast table is complete without a big bowl of bitter orange marmalade, an excellent appetizer and digestant.

Plummer F. Jones

O'Neill Arms Hotel, a typical small Irish hotel, in Toome, Co Antrim.

No Excuses

The Railway Hotel, Galway, was so vilely dirty that nothing but acute hunger forces us to remain an instant within its doors. I ask the waiter for a toothpick. 'Well, really, sor, we have none, but here's one of my own, which I'll lend yez.' In the search for it he pulls from the same pocket a dirty handkerchief and a stump of clay pipe. My laughter brings a twinkle to his eyes and procures us a much better luncheon than we had reason, from the appearance of the dirty table, to expect.

There is no excuse for this hotel. It is a disgrace to the railroad which owns and runs it. These railway hotels are generally cleanly and well kept. Certainly such is the case in England and Scotland and in the west and north of Ireland. But in Galway the broken-down, dilapidated, and filthy state of affairs is disgusting in the extreme. One hesitates to eat anything which comes from the kitchen, and we confine ourselves to boiled ham and cheese.

Michael Myers Shoemaker

Portrush Resort

At Portrush, however, there was merriment and music to spare. An approach toward rowdyism on the part of some gay young fellows was instantly checked by the watchful constabulary. The current of life was running strong. A dance was in full swing in a large hall. A theatrical performance was being given in an open air theatre down on the strand. A Stentor of righteousness was stationed at a street corner preaching repentance to a crowd of respectful listeners, and reminding them in unequivocal language of the judgment to come. Thousands of people were gathered about an open square in the centre of which was a large band stand. A concert was in progress, and the music was of a most excellent order, as the constant applause indicated.

All the essential features of a popular up-to-date coast resort are to be found at Portrush, and I doubt not that many good folks find health and happiness amid the festivities of the town and in the ocean breezes that sweep the rocky shores.

William Charles O'Donnell

The Perfect Holiday Resort

A more perfect place of holiday resort than Dugort it would not be possible to imagine. There are firm yellow sands, where children may make their mimic dykes and fortresses; mountains of moderate height, Slieve Crooghaun 2500 feet, Slievemore of only 2200, for the young and vigorous to ascend; easy hill foot-tracks for the weaker brethren; fishing either in smooth or in rolling water for those who love the indolent rocking or the rough rise and fall of the sea; precipitous and fretted cliffs carved with the likeness of some time-eaten Gothic fane by the architectonic ocean; rides, drives, and walks, amid the finest scenery of the kingdom. 'I think she prefers Brighton,' said a

Portrush station, Co Antrim, 1903, with jaunting cars in forecourt. Designed by Berkeley Deane Wise, chief engineer of the Belfast and Northern Counties Railway, it was opened in 1893.

Dugort, Achill Island, Co Mayo. Here can be seen the remains of a small Protestant mission, led by the Rev Edward Nangle, who established his 'colony' there from 1834. It was a centre of religious controversy for several decades thereafter.

stranger to me of his companion; and, if one prefers Brighton, one knows where to go. But if Nature, now majestically serene, now fierce and passionate, be more to you than bicyclettes and German bands, you can nowhere be better than at Achill, and starting from London you can be there in less than twenty-four hours. If you elect to sleep in Dublin, two easy journeys in full daylight will take you there.

Alfred Austin

DUBLIN IN THE EVENING

Fine broad streets, with fairly-good three-storied houses, swarm with people dawdling on the pavement in front of the closed shops – no cafés, few lights, ragged and barefooted urchins calling out in shrill voices the 'extra special' of the evening newspapers. Going straight on, we come upon streets deserted, silent, badly lit, with a vanishing perspective of low and dark house fronts. If it were not for the heavy and measured tread of a policeman on his beat, we might as well be in a city turned to stone. The sight of a great flare of gas, accompanied with the sound of voices, attracts us to a corner further on. Good! here we can see, at all events, though the sight is hardly a pleasant one. These festive lights illuminate public-houses like those in

England; places which are nothing more than 'gin-shops' of the lowest order. Huddled together like a flock of sheep, the customers of these wretched places drink standing about, leaning on the counter, or up against the wall, in an atmosphere poisoned by alcoholic vapours, thick with tobacco smoke, and reeking with the exhalations of foul humanity. . . .

. . . The first acquaintance is better made in the freshness of the early morning; but in Dublin the chances are that if you are up too early you will find the whole town still asleep. In the middle of summer at eight o'clock in the morning, shutters are closed and streets empty; towards nine people are beginning to wake up, maid-servants lazily sweep out the doorsteps, and shops are leisurely opened, though you can rarely find anyone ready to serve you before ten. . . . The *Trams* are empty at these early hours. These conveyances were first called *Outram-cars*, from the inventor, they are now abbreviated to *'Trams*. In Dublin there are no other omnibuses. Numberless lines of them radiate in all directions. Almost all of them start from the Central Post Office, an ostentatious building in the Grecian style, whose pediment is surmounted by statues of Hibernia, Mercury and Fidelity. It is told of a stranger that, on asking his driver what these three figures represented, he received the unhesitating answer, 'The Twelve Apostles!' and on his observing that the numbers did not tally, 'I will explain it to your honour', was the reply.

Dublin: Carlisle Bridge and Sackville Street. Here was an obvious place for a statue (begun 1864, completed 1882) to commemorate the Liberator, Daniel O'Connell, and the bridge was known as O'Connell Bridge thereafter, though not officially re-named until the mid-nineteen twenties, in the aftermath of independence.

General view of the ancestral home in Conagher townland, Dervock, Co Antrim, of William McKinley (1843–1901), 25th President of the United States of America (1897–1901).

'They only go out three at a time, turn and turn about.' This is a good specimen of popular wit. . . .

I do not believe there is another city in the world that possesses at its very gates a public park of such size, and such rare beauty. In the space of rather more than 17,000 acres of gently undulating land, there are woods of splendid elms, and copses of pink-and-white thorn, whose gnarled trunks grow to an immense size; meadows carpeted with golden-eyed daisies, on which are browsing lovely dun-coloured cows, grey sheep with black faces, and pretty little spotted fallow deer, almost tame; a zoological garden, a flower garden with trees and exotic plants and carefully-kept flower borders with the regulation rockwork, and the artificial lake tenanted by Barbary ducks; a manoeuvring and parade ground, polo and football grounds; the summer residences of the Lord-Lieutenant and the Secretary of the State for Ireland; the Irish Military College, Royal Military Hospital, artillery and police barracks. Phoenix Park contains everything but pedestrians, and it is no doubt owing to its enormous size that is has this deserted look.

Madame de Bovet

MCKINLEY'S HOME

County Antrim occupies the Northeast corner of the rhomboidal island, and is the stronghold of Protestantism and prosperity. There

Protestants outnumber Catholics three to one. There homes are happy, farms are large, fields are grain laden, cities are clean, factories are busy, schools are plentiful, churches are popular, and the people intelligent, industrious and contented. The journey to Belfast across the full length of this favored country gives abundant evidence of these pleasing conditions. The American traveler is expected to be profoundly interested in the announcement that this is the ancestral home of the McKinley's. William McKinley, President, was the son of William who was the son of James who was the son of David, whose father emigrated from the village of Conagher in the year 1743.

William Charles O'Donnell

THE ARAN ISLANDS

I am in Aranmor, sitting over a turf fire, listening to a murmur of Gaelic that is rising from a little public-house under my room.

The steamer which comes to Aran sails according to the tide, and it was six o'clock this morning when we left the quay of Galway in a dense shroud of mist.

A low line of shore was visible at first on the right between the movement of the waves and fog, but when we came further it was lost sight of, and nothing could be seen but the mist curling in the rigging, and a small circle of foam. . . .

In about three hours Aran came in sight. A dreary rock appeared at first sloping up from the sea into the fog; then, as we drew nearer, a coast-guard station and the village.

A little later I was wandering out along the one good roadway of the island, looking over low walls on either side into small flat fields of naked rock. I have seen nothing so desolate. Grey floods of water were sweeping everywhere upon the limestone, making at times a wild torrent of the road, which twined continually over low hills and cavities in the rock or passed between a few small fields of potatoes or grass hidden away in corners that had shelter. Whenever the cloud lifted I could see the edge of the sea below me on the right, and the naked ridge of the island above me on the other side. Occasionally I passed a lonely chapel or schoolhouse, or a line of stone pillars with crosses above them and inscriptions asking a prayer for the soul of the person they commemorated.

I met few people; but here and there a band of tall girls passed me on their way to Kilronan, and called out to me with humorous wonder, speaking English with a slight foreign intonation that differed a good deal from the brogue of Galway. The rain and cold seemed to have no influence on their vitality, and as they hurried past me with eager laughter and great talking in Gaelic, they left the wet masses of rock more desolate than before.

John M. Synge

QUEENSTOWN; A VERY FITTING NAME

. . . on Great Island, built into the hillside, its streets rising in tiers and in the center its rich Gothic Cathedral, one hundred and fifty feet above the shore line, was the crescent city, Queenstown.

In my ignorance I had expected to find at Queenstown something of the bang and bustle, the confusion and the grime of a modern seaport metropolis. Instead I found an almost ideal watering place, equable and sedative in climate, picturesque in location, graceful in pose, restful in spirit, healthful, contented, clean, somewhat quaint, and quite diminutive, with a population hardly numbering ten thousand.

On the third day of August 1849, the young and beloved Victoria first set foot on Irish territory, landing on the Quay amid the crashing music of military bands and the joyous booming of guns. Very fittingly the name of the city was thereupon changed from Cove to Queenstown.

William Charles O'Donnell

THE STRANGEST TRIP

Killarney

It was just 4.30 by my watch as we started from Cork on that eventful 11th day of July. There was good daylight, but the city was still wrapped in its slumbers.

It was a beautiful summer morning and our spirits rose with the aeroplane. We began the strangest trip through Ireland that was ever made by man. I can never forget the sight of the green fields of County Cork that morning. It was a scene of peaceful loveliness. . . .

. . . All at once Mike startled me again.

'In the name of all that is great, look there,' he exclaimed.

Never can I forget the sight that lay before us as I lowered my eyes and caught my first glimpse of the Vale of Killarney. The panorama was one of surpassing loveliness. There was no fear whatever in my heart now. All was wonder, admiration, delight. The three Killarney lakes lay embosomed among the towering hills. The Lakes are fully eleven miles long and at one place two and a half miles broad. Magnificent forests fringe them on every side, and over sixty wooded islands float in the charmed waters.

Harry Ferguson's Mark 1 Aeroplane, with elastic undercarriage, c. 1909. He was the first to build and fly an aeroplane in Ireland (December 1909).

County Kerry

As we winged our way above the railroad ties we rested after the excitement of Killarney. We were now in the heart of Kerry. This part of Ireland is not as prosperous as some other parts. The land is hilly and rocky. Fences are generally made of stone. The little cottages are also built of stone, thatched with straw. We could see the stack of peats beside them to be used as fuel, and the little potato patch which furnished food. Blue smoke was beginning to curl in the air from some of these cabins, telling us that rural Ireland was awakening for another day of life, such as it is.

Connemara

A few miles from Galway we turned west into the heart of the far-famed Connemara country. As we swept over this part of Ireland we could see why Connemara is so celebrated. It makes a splendid panorama. There are literally hundreds of little lakes, there is grand mountain scenery, there are the heather and peat lands in abundance.

We were glad to fly over it, however, rather than live there, for the monotony and barren soil repel a man with an active mind and a good stomach.

Men were scarce, but we saw some, mostly at work in the peat lands. We caught sight of some Connemara women also, with red skirts, and Mike said he thought they were shoeless.

We went through the pass of Kylemore, called the 'Gem of Connemara'. Two lofty peaks rise on each side, and, in order to avoid land currents, we had to rise to a height of 500 feet in going through.

I was astonished to see in this out-of-the-way place a magnificent country home. It was surrounded with an immense garden, and the walks and drives were beautified with flaming red fuchsia hedges.

I hastily referred to my little guide book, and found it was Kylemore Castle.

Alexander Corkey

POWER, INDUSTRY, ABILITY

Belfast is the center of a great manufacturing district. Each factory is surrounded by groups of neat two-storey brick cottages, with gardens, churches, schoolhouses, and shops, which are very different from the rest of Ireland, . . . every man you meet tells you that a hundred years ago Belfast had

Belfast: Castle Junction, looking down Royal Avenue. A seaport and market town of some 20,000 at the start of the nineteenth century, Belfast had grown to a dynamic industrial city port of almost 350,000 by 1900, textile, engineering and shipbuilding trades accounting for one third of its workforce.

Whitehead, Co Antrim, from the Banks. This was one of the possible points of arrival for a tunnel project, much discussed in the late nineteenth century, to join the North of Ireland with Scotland, at Portpatrick, Wigtownshire.

only fifteen thousand population, while to-day it has nearly four hundred thousand; that its wealth has doubled six times in the last twenty-five years; that it has the largest shipyards, the largest tobacco factory, the largest spinning mills, and the largest rope walk in the world. When they take you up on the side of a high mountain and show you a view of the city spread out on both sides of the River Lagan, they defy you to count the chimneys and the church spires, which are as numerous as the domes of Moscow. Belfast is the most prosperous place in Ireland and an example of matchless concentration of power, industry, and ability.

The people have good ground for their vanity, and while their claims are somewhat exaggerated, few cities have so much to boast of. One of the shipyards . . . built the first turbine that ever floated on the ocean, and together they employ fifteen thousand hands. The machine shops of Belfast are also famous. They provide spinning and weaving machines for all the linen mills in the world, and ship them even to the United States. The engines, boilers, and other machinery that is turned out from the shops of Belfast are shipped to every corner of the world, and the product of the linen factories' trade now amounts to more than sixty million dollars a year. The largest mill covers five acres, with 60,000 spindles, 1,000 looms, and more than 4,000 hands. A single tobacco firm pays $4,000,000 in taxes every year and a distillery has an annual output of $7,500,000.

Belfast has sixteen factories for the production of ginger ale, lemonade, soda, and other aërated waters, which are famous the world over. It manufactures agricultural implements and machinery for every kind of industry, and much of the machinery is the invention of its own citizens. . . .

. . . the largest part of the business as well as the sympathies of the people are with the Scots. Since the tunnel under the Hudson River has been completed between New York and Hoboken, the plan for an 'under sea railway' between Larne and Port Patrick has been revived. The engineers have reported that they can make a tunnel from Ireland to Scotland, less than forty-five miles, one hundred and fifty feet below the sea level, at a cost of $60,000,000, and some day, perhaps, it will be possible to cross by train under the Irish Channel, rather than by boat over it.

William Eleroy Curtis

AN ENGLISHMAN IN IRELAND

. . . Belfast is big, but not too big for local gossip. It has not yet succeeded in knocking the character out of individuals by making them into units. It is as proud of its City Corporation as English villagers were once proud of their parish councils. Having voted £300,000 for the construction of its new City Hall, it lavishly spent nearly double that sum so as to make the interior resplendent with marble and fresco. . . .

Yet it is curious how distinctive an impression it can leave on the memory. Doubtless it is the human element which gives it its character, and allowance must be made for the fact that in spite of its vastness Belfast has retained something of the charm, the almost personal quality, which belongs even to the ugliest of villages or rural towns. . . . One feels that the personal equation counts for so much more than it does in Liverpool. If you go into a hotel or a shop you are met not by

Patrick Street, Cork. Ireland's second city at the begining of the nineteenth century, Cork had been overtaken by Belfast in terms of population and trade long before 1900, when its population stood at 76,000 (down from its peak of 85,000 in 1851).

a mere attendant, but by a human being; you are not treated with deference, but with zeal and an inoffensive geniality. . . . You see a smiling crowd, a crowd that seems to be interested in what it is doing, to be energetic from choice or impulse and not from necessity. I heard some one comment on the fact that there are an unusual number of pretty women to be seen in the streets, the truth being, I believe, that there is no upper-class monopoly of good looks among the Irish.

R.A. Scott-James

A Cheerful City

Cork is a neat but an ugly town, which had a hundred thousand population twenty years ago and now has only eighty thousand. The missing ones, they tell me, have gone to the United States. It is one of the most prosperous and one of the cleanest cities in Ireland, and, although in former years strangers complained of pestiferous beggars, we have not seen a single one. The common people are much better dressed and the children are much neater in their appearance than those of the similar class in Dublin. They don't buy their clothing at a slopshop. They are more cheerful and happy, and the women show more pride and better taste in in their apparel. . . .

All tourists like Cork. It is a cheerful city. The atmosphere is brighter and the streets are more attractive than in Dublin. The shops are large and the show windows are well dressed, and on St. Patrick's Street, which, of course, is the principal thoroughfare, there are several windows full of most appetizing buns and cakes and other things to eat. But the tradesmen are remarkably late about getting around in the morning. When I go out for my walk after breakfast, between eight and nine o'clock, most of the shops are still closed, the doors are locked, and the shutters are up. None of the retail merchants expect customers until after nine, and then they open very slowly. The markets do not commence business until nine o'clock and wholesale dealers and their clerks do not get down until ten. A gentleman of whom I inquired about this indolent custom declared that it was as ancient as the ruins of Fin-Barre Abbey. He declared, however, that although they lie abed late in the morning the business men of Cork made things hum when they once got started.

Cork is a city of churches and some of them are modern, which is a novelty. The Roman Catholic Cathedral is an imposing structure and the interior is magnificent.

One of the 'Godless colleges' is in Cork – Queen's College – which occupies a beautiful situation upon a bluff on the outskirts of the city, entirely hidden among venerable trees and flowering plants, with a swift flowing brook at its feet.

William Eleroy Curtis

HAZARDS OF THE ROAD

On one of the first tours on which he took me we travelled to a town in the west, whence we had to motor to several places in the neighbourhood. It was my first experience of that part of Ireland, motor-cars were quite unknown, the country was very sparsely populated, and the people most unsophisticated. We had not left the station many miles behind us when we overtook a farmer driving one of the two-wheeled country carts, consisting of slabs laid upon some cross-boards. It was drawn by a typical Irish horse, showing a lot of quality and looking as if he might give a very good account of himself in an English hunting country. In the cart were various agricultural implements. After we got past I heard the most tremendous clatter and shouting, and looking round I saw that the horse had bolted and was rapidly approaching us. We, of course, pulled on one side, and stopped to see if we could be of any assistance. Before the cart reached us, all the implements and the boards of the cart had tumbled into the road. The horse shook himself clear of the harness, such as it was, jumped out of the road and proceeded to career over the adjoining fields. As if by magic, men, women, children appeared suddenly from all over the place, and proceeded to chase the

horse. I was very much alarmed that the unfortunate accident would bring down the reverse of blessings on the new Chief Secretary's head. I went back to the man and said how sorry I was at what had happened. He stood in the road watching the neighbours hunting the horse, and his only remark was: 'Well, now, isn't that a foine hunt entoirely?' After expressing my regret at causing him so much inconvenience, I offered him a modest present to atone for his trouble. He looked at it in ecstasy and said: 'Begorro! I wish this'd happen ivery day!'

Walter Long

STANLEY WILSON – MOTOR-BIKER

Stanley was a cadet member of that Wilson family who owned the Doagh Flax Spinning Mill, and was no linen merchant except under compulsion. He was, instead, an enthusiastic amateur mechanic of the internal combustion engine, and all his spare time was given to his novel and adored possession, a motor-cycle. This had a side-car of basket-work in which Mary made her first-ever journey by motor-power, complete with motoring cap and veil.

The hazards of the Irish side or 'jaunting' car.

Harry Ferguson (1884–1960), motor, aviation and tractor pioneer, engineer and inventor, seen here astride a Minerva motorcycle, with friends in the early 1900s.

It was soon the custom for all six young men to get somehow into or on to Stanley's motor-bike and take off for the week-end to Bridge House, where politeness induced Aunt Laetitia to make them welcome even as she eyed them askance. Mary, who should have had sense by now, went off into her old giggles at the picture of Stanley, still shaking violently from the prolonged vibration of his machine, graciously taking the tremulous finger-tips Aunt Laetitia extended to him, and they both shook together in a way that was unintentional.

Florence Mary McDowell

A TOUR IN IRELAND, SEPTEMBER 1905

Unofficial Notes by the Vice-President, L.G.B. (Ireland)

In an appendix to his book, Walter Long included notes of a trip to the West of Ireland in September 1905, compiled by Sir Henry Robinson, Vice-President of the Local Government Board. These extracts indicate the hazards of early motoring experienced by the veritable cavalcade of cars utilized by the official party during its two-week tour which included 'Fast Lady' (driven by Sir Henry himself), 'The Clement', the less flatteringly named 'Bathing Machine', 'Wilful Murder', and 'The Gleaner', and the more prosaic '16–20' and '10–12' models.

Tuesday. Difficulty in finding the road, Kilkenny main roads being undistinguishable from country lanes. . . .

Crossing Waterford Bridge, the 'Fast Lady', who had hitherto behaved irreproachably, kicked off her steering gear as a protest at being driven fast over a loose plank; the back wheels were promptly jammed with the brake, but the car could not be stopped in time, and dashed into the parapet, tearing a tyre open, but fortunately doing no damage to anyone. . . .

A diversion was caused by Kit dashing over the bridge on his car without being aware that toll had to be paid. . . .

After about twenty miles the 'Bathing Machine' punctured. Lady Doreen resisted all offers to be sent on, and sat on the roadside and encouraged the puncture menders. A long time thus spent, and ten minutes later another puncture occurred.

Wednesday. Outside Rathmore the 'Fast Lady' burst a new tyre beyond repair, and was left in the yard of Mr O'Sullivan's public-house, and a new tyre telegraphed for. . . .

A most perilous moonlight drive along the Loo Bridge road, headed by Kit on the 16–20, with a young constable we picked up at Headford who thought he knew the road. 'Keep the tallygraff posts forninst ye if ye can see thim, and if ye can't don't moind thim but just shtick to the road', were his instructions.

Thursday. Chief came to the door to see us off, and the 'Wilful Murder' saluted him with a startling *feu de joie* of explosions.

An appalling experience of breakdowns – not necessary to particularize, as everything went wrong which could do so. Finally the car refused to go any way except backwards, and as her back was against the gable of a house, it was obvious that either the house had to be pulled down or the car left where it was.

Got to Killarney for tea, and found our party enthusiastic over a successful boating excursion on the lakes.

Friday. Mud very bad in Abbeyfeale. Cars scarcely under control and domestic animals numerous and obstructive. The result was that the souls of a dog and several chickens ascended the Golden Stair.

Saturday. A day of skidding. The 'Bathing Machine' went backwards and sideways, any way but straight, and McCombie's smile as it rubbed along the demesne wall of

Adare Manor with two wheels in the ditch was singularly mirthless. Tea at Limerick and on by the banks of the Shannon, a very picturesque road, but dangerous on account of deep ruts, mud and the absence of fences.

Sunday. Visited Kylemore Castle, and on our way to Leenane the ignition of Kit's car went wrong. The Clement came on to break the news to us, and we sent it back to take up Kit's passengers, as we were due to lunch at Westport House at 1.30. . . .

After a good lunch with the Sligos, we started for Mulranny. Extraordinary incident in passing through the Home Farm. A sheep tried to get across the road. Finding it could not head the car, as we were going about twenty miles an hour, it put on a terrific spurt and jumped clean over the car, just touching the lamp near the bonnet with its hind feet.

Monday. Wire received after dinner from Kit and Monteith saying the 'Pom-Pom' had broken down outside Sligo, and they would stop for repairs and be with us early next morning.

Friday. Tour has been rather a severe trial for the cars, owing to rough roads, broken stones and stiff hills. To-day it was the survival of the fittest. The 'Bathing Machine' succumbed first outside Portrush, having slipped the first speed pinion.

The 'Pom-Pom', after Kit and Noonan had decorated the road with the whole of its inside, in a vain attempt to prove the mystery of its failure, suddenly broke its driving shaft, and had to be left with Noonan in a farm-yard.

Visited the Giant's Causeway, and were met by Lord Macnaghten and party; afterwards got into trouble by taking a wrong turn. . . .

Sir Henry Robinson

HEADING FOR THE HILLS

Before long we were dressed, breakfasted, and in the cab on our way to the Great Northern Railway station in Belfast. There was the fussing for tickets, the fussing for a porter, the search for a carriage in which we might remain undisturbed, the guard's long whistle, and we were off as the dawn mists were still rising from the fields. Two changes no less! and, while we waited at Clones station, a big hot cup of tea and great shiny brown buns with currants in them. Then the second change at Enniskillen where we boarded the narrow-gauge Sligo, Leitrim and Northern Countries train for Blacklion.

Now we were running through some of the loveliest country on earth; by Lough Erne through the bracken-covered, heather-covered hills of Fermanagh past Upper Lough Macnean and the Hanging Rock to Blacklion, where we were met by my uncle and the jaunting car. I have never forgotten alighting at this station, seeing the wild hills of Ireland all around, and the sight and smell of the blue turf-smoke as it rose lazily from the village chimneys.

W. Houghton Crowe

Ferry across the Lower Bann, Ulster's longest river, running from the Mourne Mountains, through Lough Neagh, to the North Antrim coast.

A passenger runs for the train at Ballindrait Station (between Lifford and Raphoe), Co Donegal, c. 1910.

'ARE YE RIGHT THERE, MICHAEL?'

A Lay of the Wild West Clare

You may talk of Columbus's sailing
  Across the Atlantical sea
But he never tried to go railing
  From Ennis as far as Kilkee.
You run for the train in the mornin',
  The excursion train starting at eight,
You're there when the clock gives the warnin',
  And there for an hour you'll wait.

(Spoken):
  And as you're waiting in the train,
  You'll hear the guard sing this refrain:–

'Are ye right there, Michael? are ye right?
Do you think that we'll be there before the night?
  Ye've been so long in startin',
  That ye couldn't say for sartin'–
Still ye might now, Michael, so ye might!'

They find out where the engine's been hiding,
  And it drags you to sweet Corofin;
Says the guard, 'Back her down on the siding,
  There's the goods from Kilrush comin' in.'

Perhaps it comes in in two hours,
  Perhaps it breaks down on the way;
'If it does,' says the guard, 'be the powers,
  We're here for the rest of the day!'

(Spoken):
  And while you sit and curse your luck,
  The train backs down into a truck!

Are ye right there, Michael, are ye right?
Have ye got the parcel there for Mrs White?
  Ye haven't! Oh, begorra!
  Say it's comin' down to-morra–
And it might now, Michael, so it might!'

At Lahinch the sea shines like a jewel,
  With joy you are ready to shout,
When the stoker cries out, 'There's no fuel,
  And the fire's taytotally out.
But hand up that bit of a log there–
  I'll soon have ye out of the fix;
There's a fine clamp of turf in the bog there;'
  And the rest go a-gatherin' sticks.

(Spoken):
  And while you're breakin' bits of trees,
  You hear some wise remarks like these:–

'Are ye right there, Michael? are ye right?
Do ye think that ye can get the fire to light?'
  'Oh, an hour you'll require,
  For the turf it might be drier—'
'Well, it might now, Michael, so it might!'

Kilkee! Oh, you never get near it!
  You're in luck if the train brings you back,
For the permanent way is so queer, it
  Spends most of its time off the track.
Uphill the ould engin' is climbin',
  While the passengers push with a will;
You're in luck when you reach Ennistymon,
  For all the way home is down-hill.

(Spoken):
  And as you're wobbling through the dark,
  You hear the guard make this remark:–

'Are ye right there, Michael? are ye right?
Do you think that ye'll be home before it's light?'
  'Tis all dependin' whether

The ould engin' howlds together—'
'And it might now, Michael, so it might!'

Percy French

A MEMORABLE EXPERIENCE

An electric tramway, the first to be built in the British Isles or elsewhere, runs along the coast from Portrush to the Giant's Causeway, a distance of about eight miles. The ride may be counted as one of the memorable experiences of a lifetime. It lies along the edge of the rugged cliffs rising high from the sea and affording a distant view across the waters. The white of the chalk exposures forms a charming color scheme with the blues and grays of the water below and the rich green of the verdure above. The incessant waves have chiseled, bored and slashed the cliffs into fantastic outlines, curious caves, tunnels and arches. The elements have there elaborated a wild architecture beyond the reach of all canons of art, mightier in its sweep and grander in execution than that of fame cathedrals of Spain and Italy.

The construction of Lifford Railway Bridge (The Foyle viaduct), Co Dongal, for the Strabane and Leterkenny Railway, the last link, serving Convoy and Raphoe, in the extensive Donegal narrow gauge network. The line was built between 1904 and 1909.

The Giant's Causeway, Co Antrim, showing the Grand Causeway from the sea. First publicised by the Royal Geographical Society in 1693 as one of the great wonders of the natural world, it remains a remarkable tourist attraction. It is recorded that Samuel Johnson thought it 'worth seeing' but not 'worth going to see'.

Dunluce Castle crowns a rocky precipice about half way between Portrush and Giant's Causeway. Considering its size, location and general aspect as viewed from a short distance, it is the most astounding castle ruin I have ever seen, not excepting the storied piles of the Rhine. Separated from the mainland by a deep and dangerous gully, the deserted walls linger on the cheerless summit a hundred feet above the pounding sea, towers and parapets forming a sombre silhouette against a sullen sky.

William Charles O'Donnell

THE GENIAL IRISHMAN

Our minds, our hearts, our souls were full of the beautiful scenes of the Emerald Isle, when we turned towards Cork for our final flight.

Before we reached the more level land, beyond the hills of Bantry Bay, we had one of our worst experiences with the aeroplane. While crossing a very broken, and hilly stretch of country, covered with stone fences, small cabins, and mountain garden patches, without any warning, the motor again stopped suddenly.

I cried out to Mike to land at once. He was compelled to alight, for, when the motor is dead, an aeroplane is like a bird with two broken wings. With the rocky ground, stone fences,

and little garden-patches, it was the most difficult descent Mike had to make. He saved the aeroplane from a smash-up only by lighting squarely on the roof of one of the little thatched cabins. As we landed on it, a man, his wife and several children rushed out and gazed at us in silent wonder. We climbed down as best we could, and explained our plight.

. . . I talked with the owner of the cabin. He seemed cheerful and pointed out to me his potato patch, his 'food and drink'.

He told me about the mountains that could be seen from his cabin, and named several of the more important hills. I noticed that a number of the names had the 'devil' in them. One peak he called the 'devil's Needle'. Another hill, with a hollow place in its side was the 'devil's Bit'. I thought I would see if there was any Irish in him, and I said:

'His Satanic Majesty seems to own a great deal of property among these hills, judging by their names.'

'Indade he does, sor,' said this son of Erin, 'but he is like most of our landlords, he makes his headquarters in London, sor.'

I saw it was no difference where you find him, in palace, mansion, villa, cottage, cabin or even hovel, an Irishman is always the same. Everywhere you will find him genial, witty, good-natured. It must be the effect of the Irish atmosphere.

When Mike had the motor going again we soon made our ascent aloft, leaving our Irish cabiners watching us in awe.

Alexander Corkey

GOVERNANCE

Although the Act of Union, 1800, had joined the two kingdoms of Ireland and Great Britain, Ireland had retained its administrative structures in Dublin, where Dublin Castle continued to house numerous civil service departments. The Queen's Representative, the Lord Lieutenant, still lived in the Vice-Regal Lodge and the Chief Secretary remained politically responsible. However, the old pillars of Protestant ascendancy that had long held sway in the nineteenth century – the established church, the army, police, courts and legal officers at the centre, and in the localities the aristocratic county grand juries, town commissioners and closed city corporations – these had declined or been swept away entirely. By 1900 the Irish political scene had been altered completely by the unfolding democratic process, the emergence of Irish political parties expressive of the majority of the Irish people, the gradual erosion of landed central and local government power and the undermining of landlord economic well-being through rent controls and land transfer. Thus, political change, outlined in the Introduction, posed fascinating alternatives as the century ended. In 1900 the Home Rule Party was reunited under John Redmond, while organized Unionism stood once more alert, spearheaded by Edward Saunderson from the 1886 crisis to his death in 1906.

In 1900, the year of Queen Victoria's final visit to Ireland,

admittedly, Irish nationalist awakening occasioned little alarm. The structures of authority seemed secure and the prospects of economic progress seemed brighter as Irish rural regeneration and British social reform advanced. On the fringes, however, radical political voices were being raised. Among these was that of Arthur Griffith who, despairing of Ireland's supine state at the centenary of the 1798 Rising, began to co-ordinate a number of separatist groups, and to evolve his Sinn Fein policy. Proclaimed in 1905, this had been given embryonic political form by 1907. The secret Irish Republican Brotherhood, itself undergoing renewal, successfully infiltrated cultural, sporting and political groups, biding its time for more overt action. Irish labour, too, began to stir. James Connolly, soon to become the biggest name on the Irish political left, founded his Irish Republican Socialist Party in 1896, but was forced to emigrate for a time to America, in 1903, in order to earn his living. James Larkin, who arrived in 1907, was to prove more immediately successful in rousing the consciousness and the solidarity of Irish workers, mobilizing the disorganized labouring classes into his Irish Transport and General Workers Union from 1909.

At the turn of the century, therefore, Ireland's governors faced challenges of uncertain magnitude.

Kylemore Castle (Abbey) Co Galway, built by Mitchel Henry, Manchester businessman, Irish landlord and MP for Galway, 1871–85. Having built the castle for his wife, who died in 1874, Henry beggared himself thereafter carrying out improvements.

A ROYAL PRESENCE

Early in April the old Queen was wheeled on to her yacht, and on the morning of the 4th she accepted the salute of the Channel Fleet in Kingstown Harbour. At half-past eleven she went on shore. Her bonnet and parasol were embroidered with silver shamrocks and there was a bunch of *real* shamrocks pinned to her black dress. The procession of four carriages travelled from Kingstown to Dublin, and for two and a half hours the little figure bowed, backwards and forwards, acknowledging cheers such as Ireland had never given before. Some of the Irish women fell upon their knees in the roadway and cried as the Queen passed by. In their hours of allegiance the Irish were not less passionate than in their hours of indignation. They had swept in from the countryside to line the long road into Dublin. Blue-jackets and soldiers and policemen guarded her way through the towns, but in many parts of the country, 'there was scarcely a policeman or soldier' to be seen. She noted this and was pleased. She drove under an arch upon which was inscribed:

> Blest for ever is she who relied
> On Erin's honour and Erin's pride.

The Queen was very tired when she came to Viceregal Lodge. She was wheeled to the foot of the staircase in her chair and then carried up to her room, where she rested. But there was complete happiness as she wrote, 'Even the Nationalists in front of the City Hall seemed to forget their politics and cheered and waved their hats.'

The Queen stayed in Ireland for twenty-two days. On the first Saturday she drove slowly among fifty-five thousand schoolchildren in Phoenix Park. One mite called out, 'Shure you're a nice old lady', as the carriage passed, and two little girls came forward with a nosegay. There was not one harsh intrusion; not one dissentient voice to mar the scene. The Queen wrote that the cheering 'was quite overpowering'.

Hector Bolitho

SPEAKING YOUR MIND

Dear Sir, Let any Irishman, who believes the Queen's visit to Ireland to be non-political, buy the current number of *Punch*. He will there find a cartoon representing the Irish members gazing, in various attitudes of terror, at a proclamation announcing this visit, while a picture of President Kruger, who is made to look as much like a chimpanzee as possible, lies at their feet, having fallen from the shaking hands of one of them. The Irish members are made as hideous as President Kruger is made and the whole is inspired by national hatred. The advisers of the Queen have not sent into Ireland this woman of eighty-one, to whom all labours must be weariness, without good reason, and the reason is national hatred – hatred of our individual national life, and, as Mr Moore has said, 'to do the work her recruiting-sergeants have failed to do', 'with a shilling between her finger and thumb and a bag

'Hibernia. "Sure, Your Majesty, there's no place like home, and it's home ye'll be with us!"' Queen Victoria visits Ireland 4 April 1900, her first visit since 1861 and only her fourth in all.

of shillings at her girdle'; and it is the duty of Irishmen, who believe that Ireland has an individual national life, to protest with as much courtesy as is compatible with vigour.

Mr Moore has said that he leaves others to suggest a form of protest. I suggest a form. It has been announced that the Queen will leave Windsor for Ireland on April 2nd. That is a remarkable day, for on that day a hundred years ago the Act of Union, having been pushed through the Irish Parliament by bribery, was introduced into the English Parliament. 'The Articles of Union', writes John Mitchel, 'were now brought forward as terms proposed by the Lords and Commons of Ireland in the form of resolutions; and on April 2, 1800, the Duke of Portland communicated to the House of Lords a message from the King, and at the same time presented to them, as documents, a copy of the Irish address with the resolution.'

I propose that a great meeting be summoned in the Rotunda on that date to protest against the Union and to dissociate Ireland from any welcome that the Unionist or the time-server may offer to the official head of that Empire in whose name liberty is being suppressed in South Africa, as it was suppressed in Ireland a hundred years ago. I propose that Mr John O'Leary be the chairman, and that all Irish members

"OUTFLANKED, BE JABERS!"

(Another of Krüger's Commandoes in Difficulties.)

The above Pathriots after enthusiastically supporting in turn Cetewayo, the Mahdi, the Afridis, King Prempeh, the Khalifa, the Boers, and other equally attractive and respectable enemies of the Queen, have solemnly granted *their* permission to the Irish people to receive their own Queen respectfully, but "without prejudice"! Now that the Shamrock is not only permittred but directed to be worn, they will no doubt vote it "afther all an overrhated vhegetable for phorpuses av dhecoration."

The Irish Parliamentary Party views the prospect of a royal visit to Ireland.

be upon the platform. If the people are left to organise their own protest, as they did on Jubilee night, there will be broken glass and batoned crowds. The people will ask themselves, as they did on Jubilee night – 'Is it worth troubling about leaders who are afraid to lead?' And let no Irishman suppose that this is not his business. Mr Redmond, when he spoke in the House of Commons, spoke in the name of Ireland; and every Irishman who would not sell his country for an Imperialism that is but materialism, more painted and flaunting than of old, should speak his mind. Yours, etc.

W.B. Yeats, 20 March 1900

DIVIDED LOYALTIES?

Sir, Whoever is urged to pay honour to Queen Victoria tomorrow morning should remember this sentence of Mirabeau's – 'The silence of the people is the lesson of Kings' She is the official head and symbol of an empire that is robbing the South African Republics of their liberty, as it robbed Ireland of theirs. Whoever stands by the roadway

cheering for Queen Victoria cheers for that Empire, dishonours Ireland, and condones a crime.

But whoever goes to-morrow night to the meeting of the people and protests within the law against the welcome that unionists and time-servers will have given to this English Queen, honours Ireland and condemns a crime. Yours sincerely.

W.B. Yeats, 4 April 1900

A FOND FAREWELL

Viceregal Lodge, Phoenix Park,
Dublin, April 25th, 1900.

The Queen is very anxious before leaving Ireland, where she has spent a most agreeable time, to express, through the Lord-Lieutenant, to her Irish people, how very much gratified and how deeply touched she has been by her reception here. During the three weeks that the Queen has spent in this charming place she has been received by all ranks and creeds with an enthusiasm and an affection which cannot be surpassed. Each time the Queen came here before with her dear husband they were always kindly and warmly welcomed. But on this occasion, after a lapse of thirty-nine years, her reception has equalled that at her previous visits, and she carried away with her a most pleasant and affectionate memory of the time she has spent in Ireland. The Queen earnestly prays that goodwill and harmony may prevail amongst all her people and that they may be happy and prosperous.

Lord Cadogan, Viceroy, quoted in Michael J.F. McCarthy

A DIFFICULT POSITION

While not exactly a sinecure, the post of Lord-Lieutenant of Ireland was largely a shop-window one. The Chief Secretary, who, as a member of the Cabinet, spent more of his time in London than in Dublin, was the real ruler of the country, and though Mr Gladstone had once defined the relative powers of the Cabinet and the Queen's Viceroy as 'the Cabinet for policy, the Lord Lieutenant for administration,' this hard distinction did not always correspond to Dublin Castle facts. 'Mr Morley', writes Lord Aberdeen in a revealing passage of his memoirs dealing with his Viceroyalty of 1886, when John Morley was for the first time

Chief Secretary, 'being much absorbed with his share of the preparation of the Home Rule Bill, and other Parliamentary duties, was the more ready to leave matters to be dealt with at our end, and even asked me to administer his rights of patronage.' The Lord-Lieutenant had in practice to rest content with what crumbs of power the Chief Secretary let drop: Morley's tone in his correspondence with Houghton is that of an indulgent but preoccupied and imperious tutor. Moreover, the position of Lord-Lieutenant was in itself paradoxical: representing the Sovereign it was in theory the Lord-Lieutenant's duty to hold himself aloof from and above all Party politics, yet since he was also a member of the Government, his term of office limited by their tenure of power, his every action was scrutinised both by the Irish themselves and by the Parliamentary Opposition in London. 'He is in an anomalous position,' wrote Houghton, 'and no definite rule exists for his guidance. His interference in, or abstention from, politics must vary in amount according to circumstances, and for the amount he is not directly responsible to anybody. My own view is that the less he mixes in Parliamentary business the better.' Whatever the Viceroy did, whatever he did not do, he was sure to be criticised and attacked. 'It was always a mystery,' writes Lord Newton in his biography of Landsowne, 'that anyone could be found voluntarily to accept the Irish Viceroyalty.'

The Vice-regal Lodge, home of the official representative of the Crown in Ireland, in Phoenix Park, Dublin.

Dublin Castle. Dating from the thirteenth century, Dublin Castle became the seat of British administration in Ireland, retaining many of its functions even after the Union in 1801.

There was, moreover, the matter of expense. Lansdowne himself called the traditions of the office 'horribly extravagant', and complained that there was too much 'flunkeyism and parade', the Viceroy keeping up a semi-royal state with levees 'as elaborate as those held at St. James's'. . . . In those days the Dublin season was much enlivened by the presence of the battalions of the Foot Guards stationed there for duties at the Castle. The Lord-Lieutenant was expected to give many dances besides holding the state levees at which he had to kiss debutantes on the cheek. More agreeable to Houghton than any of this, there were also many race-meetings within easy reach of Dublin, at Baldoyle, Leopardstown and the Curragh – the last being both the Newmarket and the Aldershot of Ireland.

. . . Inside the Lodge and the Castle the alien court, with its English aides-de-camp and English equerries, its grooms of the chamber walking backwards, kept up its pomp in vast saloons ornamented by English royal portraits and crowded with pot-palms, occasional tables and settees. Here the Viceroy, wearing the Irish diamond insignia, reputed to be worth £20,000, round his neck, would preside in the throne room as the representative of his Sovereign. . . . Lord Houghton, who was tall and handsome, could ride a horse to perfection, sit erect in a state carriage, 'kiss a regiment of women' on presentation nights, and make a good bow, was a suitable and decorative symbol of English rule.

James Pope-Hennessy

BRIGHT FUTURES

'For a country so attractive and a people so gifted we cherish the warmest regard, and it is, therefore, with supreme satisfaction that I have during our stay so often heard the hope expressed that a brighter day is dawning upon Ireland. I shall eagerly await the fulfilment of this hope. Its realisation will, under Divine Providence, depend largely upon the steady development of self-reliance and co-operation, upon better and more practical education, upon the growth of industrial and commercial enterprise, and upon that increase of mutual toleration and respect which the responsibility my Irish people now enjoy in the public administration of their local affairs is well-fitted to teach'.

Message of the King to the Irish People, 1st August, 1903

LETTERS OF GEORGE WYNDHAM

To his Brother, 6 June 1901

. . . I have had a hard session and an interesting Whitsun. There was a row on the Dillon Estate purchased by Congested Districts Board, so I went off to Ballaghaderreen to settle it, the moment the House rose. The 'Freeman' beat up an opposition to me and two agitator M.P.s – O'Donnell and Cullinan – went to hold a rival meeting at same time and place. All, however, went off well. Their meeting was damped by the rain and I remained in possession of the field. After that I went to

Westport, embarked on the Granuaile and visited Clare Island and the Aran Isles; got caught in a gale off Slyne Head but enjoyed myself and did a good stroke of business. House meets to-morrow and I expect a stiffish two months of it. But I'm still in the saddle and got a letter yesterday from a Nationalist telling me to stick to it and not mind the agitators. Nor do I.

To his Mother, 8 August 1901

. . . Now we are having a regular old-fashioned summer holiday time framed on the model of my earlier exploits. Perf [his son] is better than for years and has constituted himself master of the ceremonies. He knows all the polo, cricket, racing and theatrical fixtures and takes care that the Chief Secretary shall make a creditable public appearance wherever the 'Fancy' and 'le Sport' are gathered together.

The day presents a wonderful blend of all the family proclivities. At 8.30 I read prayers to Sibell [his wife], the cook, and the butler. At 8.40 I ride – 'harsing in the Phanix' with Perf and Tony Shaftesbury. . . .

After my breakfast, I have up the Under-Secretary, or Vice-President of Local Government Board, etc., etc., and put in two or three hours of easy-going work. Then Percy takes me to cricket-matches, polo, Leopardstown, etc., etc. And we wind up with frantic lawn-tennis till 7.30. Dinner at eight. Perf to bed at 9.30. Then music as a rule till 12 o'clock. . . .

Meanwhile all my Departments are working on lines I have laid down to collect every proposal – whether for railways, harbours, or arterial drainage, and we shall together beat out a policy on my return.

I cross to England with Percy for Eton on 18th, and then will come to you perhaps with Sibell, shoot the following Tuesday and Wednesday as arranged, and return here Thursday 26th to work at my Land Bill.

To-morrow I have a Congested Districts Board at 9.45 a.m. and at 1.30 we all go in pomp with His Excellency, Lancer escort etc., etc., to the Horse Show. . . .

What with Horse-show, Cricket, Polo, Racing, Hospitals, Congested Districts, Lawn-tennis, Croquet, Billiards, and Ping-Pong we manage to 'keep the Tambourine a rowlin'.

George Wyndham

Edward VII at the foundation stone laying of Belfast Technical College, College Square East, on 27 July 1903.

Renmore Barrack, Galway: a staged photograph, but one showing some of the training undertaken in several such barracks by the Irish Command, amounting in 1900 to about 21,000 soldiers.

A MILITARY MAN

On non-hunting days, after morning parade, a jaunting-car, with a professional poacher in attendance, was invariably to be found waiting in the barrack square. After a hurried lunch, or with a packet of sandwiches, we would sally forth with him. The procedure was to drive about the country and under the guidance of our poacher friend, stop at any likely looking bog, get out, shoot it, and return to the car, sometimes after walking over an intervening bit of country, and thus proceeding on our way till nightfall. Then, having perhaps waited for the evening flight of duck, we would get back to barracks with a bag of probably a dozen couple of snipe, two or three brace of partridges, a couple or more of ducks and an odd hare or pheasant. . . .

The Curragh of those days was a delightful station. For a season I ran the garrison cricket club, but then became obsessed by polo, and from that time on played little cricket. We had a very good regimental team. . . .

Then from Dublin used to come big contingents, headed by the Viceroy and his staff. Lords Londonderry, Zetland and Cadogan all hunted regularly during their term of office. . . .

It was about this time that I once managed to hunt thirteen days running; the Sunday with a Land League pack near Athy, being by no means the worst of them.

An interesting feature of life at Curragh was, of course, the racing, and the numerous training stables which surrounded us. . . .

A good deal of ragging used to go on, and a favourite amusement after dinner was to 'draw' the ash-bins for a 'Curragh buck'. This was our name for the sheep who tried to supplement from the refuse the scanty fare provided by the short grass of the Curragh. These animals were very active and took a lot of stalking and catching. Once caught, they would be hurled in through a window, on the top of some unfortunate who had gone to bed. The wreckage of his room by the maddened beast can well be imagined.

It would be hard to find a greater galaxy of beauty than one saw in those days at the viceregal balls in St. Patrick's Hall at the Castle in Dublin. The Duchess of Leinster, to my mind, stood out among them all, but, of the Irish girls, Miss Priscilla Armytage Moore, Constance Gore-Booth, Nita Head, who married 'Bobby' Bower of the 60th Rifles, Mrs (now Lady) Greer, Miss Maud Gonne, the Lambart sisters from Beauparc, Lady Beatrice Butler, who married General Sir R. Pole-Carew, Lady Conyngham, Catherine Conolly, and many others held their own well among the many good looking visitors from England, and wives of officers quartered in the country.

Finance was the difficulty, and the best plan I could think of was to try and make the polo pay for the hunting. I managed to scrape up enough money to buy raw ponies, and to the training of these I proceeded to devote myself. Soldiering at a depot in those days was not taken as seriously as it is now, and presented no obstacle. Some of the ponies came out of turf carts; one of the best out of a trap from suburbs of Dublin. I was fairly successful, and sold several for good prices.

General Sir Alexander Godley

Troops in George's Street, Limerick, a town founded by the Vikings on the lowest fording point of the Shannon. The scene illustrates a feature of many Irish towns that grew up around a main street built wide enough for military deployment.

AN IRISH FIGHT

At Talana Hill (October 1899) the Blake-MacBride brigade found itself defending Boer positions against the Royal Dublin Fusiliers, so generating the ballad ''Twas an Irish Fight':

Dicey took a lad named Walsh; Dooley got McGurk
 Gilligan turned on Flaherty's boy – for his father he used
 to work.
They had marched to fight the English – but Irish were all
 they could see
 That's how the 'English fought the Dutch' at the Battle of
 Dundee

David Fitzpatrick

'LET ERIN REMEMBER'

[The following extract is taken from the Cork Examiner *of 15 January 1900. The harrowing account describes the departure for South Africa of the North Cork Militia (King's Royal Rifles) on 14 January 1900. Stationed at Templemore Barracks, Co. Tipperary, the troops were entrained and moved for embarkation on the morning of the 14th, their women folk assembling over the previous night in order to see them off, some covering the 15 miles from Cork to Queenstown on foot.]*

Any one who slept in the vicinity of the main streets of Queenstown on Friday night and the early hours of Saturday morning could have heard expressed in the peculiar wail of the poor female friends of the departing troops an affection which, if it were general, would make us very Utopian in existence. Those who could afford the price of the fare, travelled from Cork to Queenstown and a sad scene they created. On arrival at the station, they conveyed an expression of surprise that their departing friends were not there, and when they had passed out of the gate and recognised the grand troopship drawn up alongside the Deepwater Quay that was to carry their friends to a scene where uncertainty of life is painfully recognised, they set up a cry that would touch the most stoic. But sadder still is the fact that many poor female friends of the militia could not afford the price of the train fare, and they walked all the way from Cork to Queenstown. It was an exhibition of affectionate feeling one could not easily forget. They arrived in Queenstown, the most part of them, absolutely without one halfpenny, and it was only natural that they should make their presence felt in such circumstances. . . .

Drawing near noon the embarkation had been completed, and then the people got their way. They rushed in on the quay, and those who witnessed the scene will not easily forget it. Youngsters climbed up on the lamps to get a glimpse of their relatives, while it was feared that some of the women would fall into the river, so anxious were they all to see their relatives. There were shouts of 'Good-bye' as the steamer

Group seated around a poteen still. The illicit production of the 'eau de vie' of the country was still widespread at this time.

moved off, and was being cleverly turned in the stream by the pilot, Mr James Nash, within her own length from the guardship *Howe*, and the band struck up selections of 'The Soldiers of the Queen', 'The Girl I Left Behind Me' and 'Auld Lang Syne', while the guardship band rendered as the *Nile* was turning 'Let Erin Remember'. But the men heeded not the music, their hearts were too fully expressed in their features. They seemed sad, not through fear of an engagement, we know, but they felt they were badly wanted at home, where their relatives will now have to struggle on a miserable pittance. It was a scene to make one turn away and feel sorry that such a thing could be possible, because we saw one woman, who, in sheer desperation at the departure of her two sons, stretched herself on the ground and scraped the earth until the blood flowed from her hands. The Angelus bell had not rung when the grand steamer made its way out of the harbour amidst a wail that seemed like a sound of a 'great Amen'. Major McCalmont stated that he never saw a more orderly crowd of men, and there were expressions of admiration by Englishmen at the physique of the men. . . .

In reference to the way in which it has been stated the North Cork volunteered it should be understood that the men when on parade were not asked if they would go on duty at the Cape. They were told that they were expected to do duty at some foreign station. It now remains for our so-called loyal people who boast so much about doing work for Queen and country, but never do anything, to come to the aid of the poor people who were dependent on the members of the North Cork Rifles for their maintenance.

POLICEMAN AND POTEEN MAKERS

The sergeant was in charge of the station. Generally in that station the strength was one sergeant and four constables, and his job was to run the station as it should be run, attend to the patrolling of the district, see it was properly and adequately patrolled both by day and by night, and that all complaints were attended to, promptly attended to. There was very little crime, very little crime, the police time was taken up principally by what they call 'still hunting' – running after poteen makers. There was very, very little crime. No serious crime, none, and the people all lived as good neighbours together.

I remember one search for poteen. He was after seizing a worm, you know the worm that's attached to the still. He found where the man was working and arrested the man. When they were coming down along the mountain he was wondering where the still was, you see, he got the worm but he didn't get the still. Coming down the mountain in under a shrubbery he saw the still lying, where it had been hidden and he pointed it out to the man that had only been arrested. The man says, 'well I couldn't tell you sergeant who throwed her in the bush'.

There was quite a lot of poteen making in Glencolumbkille. They called the whiskey that you bought in the shops the Parliament Whiskey, it wasn't strong enough for a lot of the men in those days. There were no evictions or problems over land in Glencolumbkille, but further down on the Donegal coast they had evictions at which my father had to attend. That was where there was a District Inspector murdered, he was at those evictions [perhaps the death of District Inspector Martin, killed by a crowd while attempting to arrest Rev. McFadden at Gweedore in 1889]. The police didn't carry out any part of the evictions, they were only there to protect the bailiffs. The police weren't allowed to put their hands on anything, to remove anything from a house, or seize, simply to preserve the peace, that was their duty there and that's what they stuck to. He did not like the duty at all but he had no option.

They had guns in the Barracks, you see, each man had a carbine in the Barracks, probably, they had to do, you see, some Barracks were attacked in those days and they had it for the defence of Barracks, for carrying out important escort duty or something like that. Normally on patrol work all they carried was just the waist belt, handcuffs and baton. That's what my father carried, the waist belt, handcuffs and baton in the case, that was the equipment for those days.

John D. Brewer

CLANDEBOYE'S TREASURE

The outer hall at Clandeboye (since my uncle possessed acquisitive instincts and had travelled much) was filled with many loveable objects. The steps which led down to the front door were flanked by a double row of curling stones from Scotland and from Canada, some of which bore silver plaques commemorative of curling triumphs at Inverary or at Montreal. To the left of these unwieldy playthings stood an enormous block of Egyptian granite carved with the semblance of the cow-headed Hathor and bearing the ibis cartouche of Thutmosis I. Balanced upon this pink monolith was the stuffed and startled head of a rhinoceros. In the plaster of the left wall were embedded a series of Greek inscriptions picked out in red paint. These, when I became old enough to decipher them, proved to be little more than the play-bills of the time, announcing to Thebes or Eleusis the impending performance of some now unknown trilogy. Beyond these inscriptions a Russian bear raised enormous paws. On the right hand of the entrance, a mummy case, two cannon, a Burmese bell slung between carved figures, and a second bear of smaller dimensions, were artistically grouped; the wall behind them had been covered with wire netting on which were affixed dirks, daggers, cutlasses, pistols, lances, curling brooms, and a collection of those neat little fly-whisks with which the acolytes dust the high altar of St Peter's at Rome.

The inner hall was larger and more deliberately baronial. It was lit by a vast tudor window bearing the arms and quarterings of the Blackwoods and the Hamiltons. There

Eviction scene, possibly on the Vandeleur estate, Co Clare, in the 1890s. Though no longer a central feature of Irish rural life by 1890, evictions still occurred, involving, as here, all the forces of law and order: police, military, magistrate and landlord's agent.

Clandeboye House, Co Down, a late Georgian house designed by Robert Woodgate, and home of Frederick, Lord Dufferin, later Marquis of Dufferin and Ava, Governor General of Canada, 1872–8, Viceroy of India, 1884–8, the foremost imperial administrator of the late Victorian era.

Helen's Tower, in the grounds of Clandeboye House, home of the Marquis of Dufferin and Ava, a memorial completed in 1862 by Lord Dufferin to commemorate his mother, Helen, Lady Dufferin. The subject of poetic tributes, including one by Tennyson, it would itself be used as the model for the memorial at Thiepval (Somme) to the 16th Ulster Division, slaughtered at the battle of the Somme in 1916.

flamed the cap of maintenance and the scarlet crescent. There blazed the heraldic tiger ermine and the flags of Burmah charged with a peacock in its pride proper. There glittered the stars and collars of the Indian Empire, St Patrick and the Bath. And there also shone the simpler emblems of the Hamilton family. That bleeding heart. That gentle antelope; on this occasion *affronté*, ermine, attired and unguled.

Harold Nicolson

HELEN'S TOWER

Helen's Tower, here I stand,
Dominant over sea and land,
Son's love built me, and I hold
Mother's love engraved in gold.
Love is in and out of time;
I am mortal stone and lime.

Would my granite girth were strong
As either love, to last as long!
I should wear my crown entire
To and through the Doomsday fire,
And be found in angel eyes
In earth's recurring Paradise.

Alfred Lord Tennyson

THE UNFORGIVING EARTH

What is called the Congested Districts Board was created in 1891 to improve conditions on the west coast, where the standard of living is at the lowest point and the people are in a chronic state of famine because of the inferior quality of the soil. This district consists of the province of Connaught, the counties of Donegal, Kerry, and Clare, and the districts of Bantry, Castletown, Schull, and Skibbereen in the County of Cork. The land in those localities is very poor. . . . The majority of the people live on small plots, where they manage to raise a few potatoes and cabbages and keep a few cows, goats, pigs, and sheep of worn-out breeds, which they drive wherever they can find pasturage. Most of them try to earn a little more money by going to other parts of the kingdom to work as laborers for a portion of the year or by weaving homespun, fishing, gathering seaweed, and other home industries.

The act empowers the board to aid migration to other parts of Ireland, to assist in the improvement of live stock and the breeding of horses, cattle, sheep, donkeys, and swine, to encourage poultry farms, bee-keeping, basket-making, lace-making, knitting, and the manufacture of carpets, rugs, and other things that can be made at home, and to encourage the fishing industry by constructing piers and harbors and furnishing boats and gear.

William Eleroy Curtis

A PUBLIC PROPOSAL

Dublin, 27 August 1895

Sir,

As an Irish representative I have a proposal affecting the general welfare of Ireland to make to my fellow members, and I make it publicly in order that there may be no suspicion of political intrigue, and that any Irishman who desires to do so may have an opportunity of expressing his judgement upon it.

I am opposed to Home Rule because I do not think it would be good for Ireland. Most of my colleagues are in favour of it because they think otherwise. But we are agreed that the recent elections have made it extremely improbable, so far as human foresight can tell, that Home Rule can be granted for some years to come. The majority of my colleagues believe that the National demand is indestructible and ultimately irresistible.

I do not believe that Home Rule is dead, or that it ever will be while so many of my colleagues are sent to the Imperial Parliament pledged to vote for it. I go further and admit that if the average Irish elector, who is more intelligent than the average British elector, were also as prosperous, as industrious, and as well educated, his continued demand in the proper constitutional way for Home Rule would very likely result in the experiment being one day tried. On the other hand I believe that if the material condition of the great body of our countrymen were advanced, if they were

Road-making in Donegal under the auspices of the Congested Districts Board, here providing outdoor relief employment while improving communications in an impoverished western county.

Arthur Griffith (1871–1922), founder of Sinn Fein (1906), the abstentionist, independence party, who sought a withdrawal of Irish MPs from Westminster and the establishment of an Irish parliament in Dublin.

Colonel Edward Saunderson: MP 1865–1906, leader of the Parliamentary Unionists 1888–1906.

George Russell, 'AE', (1867–1935), writer, painter, poet and mystic, and editor (1905–23) of the Irish Homestead, *journal of the Cooperative movement in Ireland.*

John Redmond (1856–1918), appointed leader of the Irish Parliamentary Party in 1900, re-uniting the factions divided by the disgrace and death of Parnell ten years earlier.

Sir Horace Plunkett(1854–1932), founder of the Cooperative movement in Ireland, politician and reformer.

EVICTED.

Sir H-r-ce Pl-nk-tt. "Well, Mr. R–dm–nd, you and D–ll–n have had your way! You've got rid of me, though I was a good friend to Ireland!"

Mr. J-hn R-dm-nd. "Ah! that is precisely your offence. You represented an alternative to *us*, so you had to go!"

encouraged in industrial enterprise, and were provided with practical education in proportion to their natural intelligence, they would see that a political development on lines similar to those adopted in England was, considering the necessary relations between the two countries, best for Ireland, and then they would cease to desire Home Rule.

. . . I therefore venture to submit a practical suggestion to my colleagues in the spirit which I have always displayed and which I have reason to believe meets with a larger measure of approval than would have been accorded when I first had the honour of Irish representation conferred upon me three years ago. I have made this suggestion in the House of Commons, and have discussed it privately with colleagues of all sections, and it has met with universal encouragement.

. . . Let the Irish Parliamentary party name three or four practical men. Let Mr John Redmond name, say, a couple,

and let us Unionists name a couple more. Let these form a Recess Committee – for the plan is so experimental it might be better to deal only with the present and the immediate future – and let these Parliamentarians have power to add to their number by unanimous or nearly unanimous selection. The selections need not be limited to M.Ps. Any practical Irishman whose opinion is of value might be invited to join.

The scope of their legislative suggestions would be decided upon by the committee. But I would submit that two pressing matters would lend themselves especially to this kind of conciliatory negotiation – a Board of Agriculture for Ireland and a Technical Education Bill. . . . If we cannot agree (and this is a most unlikely contingency) upon the details of these or other measures, we must only relegate them to the controversial shelf from which we all desire to take them down. . . .

I am, Sir,
    Your obedient servant,
(Signed),   Horace Plunkett.

THE CORK EXHIBITION, 1902

The part we took at the Cork Exhibition of 1902 was well understood in Ireland, but not perhaps elsewhere. We secured a large space both in the main Industrial Hall and in the grounds, and gave an illustration not of what Ireland had done, but of what, in our opinion, the country might achieve in the way of agricultural and industrial development in the near future. Exhibiting on the one hand our available resources in the way of raw material, we gave, on the other hand, demonstrations of a large number of industries in actual operation. These exhibits, imported with their workers, machinery and tools, from several European countries and from Great Britain, all belonged to some class of industry which, in our belief, was capable of successful development in Ireland. In the indoor part of the exhibit there was nothing very original, except perhaps in its close relation to the work of a government department. But what attracted by far the greatest interest and attention was a series of object lessons in many phases of farm activities, where, in our opinion, great and immediate improvements might be made. Here were to be seen varieties of crops under various systems of treatment, demonstrations of sheep-dipping, calf-rearing on different foods, illustrations of the different breeds of fowl and systems of poultry management, model buildings and gardens for farmer and labourer; while in separate buildings the drying and pressing of fruit and vegetables, the manufacture of butter and cheese, and a very comprehensive forestry exhibit enabled our visitors to combine profitable suggestion with, if I may judge from my frequent opportunities of observing the sightseers in whom I was particularly interested, the keenest enjoyment.

We kept at the Exhibition, for six months, a staff of competent experts, whose instructions were to give to all-comers this simple lesson. They were to bring home to our people that, here in Ireland before their very eyes, there were industries being carried on by foreigners, by Englishmen, by Scotchmen, and in some instances by Irishmen, but in all cases

A general view of the Great Exhibition, Cork, 1902/3.

by men and women who had no advantage over our workers except that they had the technical training which it was the desire of the Department to give to the workers of Ireland. The officials of the Department entered into the spirit of this scheme enthusiastically and cheerfully, some of them, in addition to their ordinary work, turning the office into a tourist agency for these busy months. With the generous help of the railway companies they organized parties of farmers, artisans, school teachers, members of the statutory committees, and, in fact, of all to whom it was of importance to give this object lesson upon the relations between practical education and the promotion of industry. Nearly 100,000 persons were thus moved to Cork and back before the Exhibition closed – an achievement largely due to the assistance given by the Irish Agricultural Organisation Society and the clergy throughout the country.

This experiment, both in its conception and in its results, was perhaps unique. There were not wanting critics of the new Department who stood aghast at so large an expenditure upon temporary edifices and a passing show; but those who are in touch with its educational work know that this novel application of State assistance fulfilled its purpose. It helped substantially to generate a belief in, and stimulate a demand for, technical instruction which it will take us many years adequately to supply.

Sir Horace Plunkett

THE GLORIOUS TWELFTH

Then the waiter, seeing we were ignorant Americans explained to us how they celebrated the victory of the Boyne every Twelfth of July, and how the celebration that day was to be the biggest ever held. Then I remembered how the great day in the North of Ireland is the Twelfth of July, just as the Seventeenth of March is the great day in the rest of Ireland. However, St. Patrick's Day is now generally observed in some way not only in Ireland, but in all the world.

'Mike,' said I, 'let us stay in Enniskillen today and celebrate.'

'We'll stay and rest,' said Mike, 'and see what they do here on the "glorious Twelfth", as our waiter calls it.'

After breakfast we went out on the streets, and found them filling up with a holiday crowd. I was reminded of a celebration of July Fourth in America. Excursion trains coming in from different points in the surrounding territory added to the crowd every hour. These excursion parties brought with them in every case one or two fife bands, and occasionally a brass band. These bands played popular airs to the great delight of the crowd. All these numerous bands, and the immense crowd of Irishmen and Irish women, gathered in a large field beside Enniskillen. It was a scene of the greatest enthusiasm. Bands in different parts of the field were playing different airs.

Ancient Order of Hibernians Band, Cloghcor, Co Tyrone (No. 463). The AOH took its modern form in the 1830s, in Ireland and New York, as a counter to the Orange Order. With its motto 'Fidelity to Faith and Fatherland' it was at its strongest in South Ulster.

Orangemen parading in the Diamond, Raphoe, Co Donegal, c. 1910. Founded in 1795 to protect Protestant interests, the Orange Order grew massively in the late nineteenth century, supporting the Union with Britain in the face of the rising demand for Irish Home Rule.

'Big Jim' Larkin (1876–1947), trade union organiser extraordinaire, representative of the British-based National Union of Dock Labourers and future creator of the Irish Transport and General Workers Union (December 1908).

All was hub-bub and excitement. There were stands all around where all kinds of drinks were sold. Already several plainly showed that they had been drinking a liquid much stronger than lemonade. Lads and lasses were walking around, jostling, crowding and laughing. It was a good-natured crowd, as there was no counter-demonstration of any kind, as happens sometimes in other parts of Ireland, I understand.

Alexander Corkey

A BELFAST WORKING MAN

It was when I was put on this regular duty that I was reminded of my father's long hours. When I studied the hours I would work each week (over 72) it was only work and sleep. I asked some of the men in the depot if we could not get these hours reduced by starting a union but no one would listen to me. I was told if the manager heard about me trying to form a union I would be dismissed. Mason my next door neighbour an old driver who knew my father warned me about the risk in talking about an organization but I had made up my mind to join one, and I interviewed the late Alex Boyd who was organizing municipal employees. I got my first card which I still have: it is dated the 11 Nov 1907. I encouraged a few others to join, but later on they took cold

Union platform during the 1907 Belfast Strike.

Urban District Council of Portadown, Co Armagh, 1899. The Irish Local Government Act of 1898 was the first to provide a local government structure on English lines and to bring democratic local government to Ireland.

feet and when I spoke to them they said their job was more important. I never lost an opportunity of trying to convince the men that they were standing in their own light.

Robert McElborough

NATIONAL INDEPENDENCE

Sinn Féin holds that, to use an old similitude, the sun of national independence alone can scatter the deep darkness that has been gathering for so long over the land, and it appeals to the gentry, to the industrial and manufacturing classes, to the society Catholic, to the Protestant Ulsterman, to abandon their ancient distrust of the nation and to unite with the rest of the Nationalist forces in setting the national house in order – or rather in building a new national house altogether. It is the first nationalist movement, I believe, which appeals directly to the middle-classes in the town centres, for its leaders realise that no great national revolution was ever yet accomplished without the aid either of an

organized upper-class or of an organized middle-class, or both. It has been criticised, on the other hand, for not appealing with a sufficiently winning voice to the artisans and labourers, but that it has not yet done so is partly due to a laudable determination to keep national solidarity and independence the sole planks in its platform and not to allow its forces to be divided on a class issue. Even social reform, it contends, cannot be radical or of much avail while an unsettled and unsettling national question troubles the air.

Many Irish men and women refrain from being Nationalists, because, they say, Ireland is too small and too poor to be an independent nation. Here again, the Sinn Féiner offers his answer – in the form of a statistical table this time. In this table, the area, population, revenue and taxation of seven more or less independent European Nations are compared with those of Ireland. The list reads as follows:

Country	Description	Area (square miles)	Population	Revenue £	Taxation per head £ s. d.		
Denmark	Independent Kingdom	15,388	2,464,770	4,250,000	1	13	0
Wurtemberg	Suzerain Kingdom	7,534	2,169,486	4,500,000	1	8	6
Greece	Guaranteed Kingdom	25,014	2,433,806	3,000,000	1	3	6
Roumania	Independent Kingdom	50,720	5,936,690	9,250,000	1	4	0
Sweden	Independent Kingdom	172,876	5,513,644	8,800,000	1	13	6
Norway	Independent Kingdom	124,129	2,240,032	5,500,000	1	12	6
Switzerland	Independent Republic	15,976	3,315,443	4,600,000	1	7	6
IRELAND		32,531	4,391,543	9,753,500	2	4	4

Robert Lynd

POLITICS AND POTATOES

A few other matters worth mentioning occurred towards the close of 1896. The tercentenary of the potato was celebrated in Dublin; and Lord Cadogan, taking part in the celebrations, informed the Irish Gardeners' Association that the Government intended to establish a Board of Agriculture for Ireland in the next session. He also told them they ought to teach people, particularly English people, how to cook a potato, as well as how to grow it.

Michael J.F. McCarthy

Chapter 3

EARNING A LIVING

*T*raditionally an agricultural country with an overwhelming 72 per cent of its people living in rural areas (defined as communities of less than 1,500 people), Ireland in 1901 supplied the British market with much dairy produce, beef, lamb and pork, some beers and spirits, a few textile items and cut-glass and leather goods. Ireland had been unable to compete with the mass production of English factories and a waning population steadily left the land, leaving too often for the cities of Britain or for countries further afield, across the Atlantic or the Pacific. In the North-east alone, successful industrialisation had created in Belfast a modern city built on linen manufacture, ship building, and the production of engineering machinery, tobacco goods and ropes. Elsewhere, in small towns and villages, rural crafts survived, though increasingly threatened by the arrival by rail of mass-produced imports.

In the poorer regions, government-sponsored road- and rail-building schemes were augmented from 1891 by craft training schemes, land redistribution, and pier and harbour building under the auspices of the Congested Districts Board. The Department of Agriculture and Technical Instruction, from its inception in 1899, established model farms, advised on crop and animal husbandry, and recommended new techniques and devices designed to improve living standards and so check the flight from the land.

The Cooperative movement, founded by Sir Horace Plunkett in 1889, initiated joint purchasing, production and marketing ventures in the interests of the producers, and made its own contribution to raising standards through its weekly journal, The Irish Homestead, founded in 1895. A year earlier, when the movement had grown to thirty-three societies, a national co-ordinating body, the Irish Agricultural Organization Society, was inaugurated. By 1904 the IAOS had 876 member societies, and Plunkett's slogan – 'Better farming, Better business, Better living' – had been widely accepted. It was land that was still at the centre of interest for many of the Irish, and this was steadily passing into the hands of those who worked it, through successive purchase legislation. This was to culminate in the 1903 (Wyndham) Act that finally found the formula by which landlords could sell and tenants could buy on a mutually advantageous basis

Already, by the 1890s, changing patterns of work had emerged. The 1891 census showed that agriculture now accounted for only 44.4 per cent of the employed workforce (though there were many more living on farms who were classified as unproductive, for example, 'relatives assisting'), with the manufacturing industry at 17.8 per cent, domestic service 12.2 per cent, industrial service 6.6 per cent, and the public and professional services totalling 5.8 per cent. The transport sector, reflecting the modernising processes, stood at 2.6 per cent, on a par with building.

The thrust of all this activity, allied to increased literacy and communication, was to enhance political awareness, a sense of national distinctiveness and an enthusiasm for Irish management of Irish affairs, whether in the form of Home Rule or, in more extreme circles, complete repeal of the Act of Union and full independence.

Flax retting: removing flax from a lint hole, Co Antrim. Fortunately the vile smell of this part of the linen process has not been preserved by the camera.

LETTERS FROM AE

To Katharine Tynan Hinkson

22 Lincoln Place
Dec. 19th 1901

Dear Mrs Hinkson,

I have just returned from the country and have time to jot down a few ideas about Horace Plunkett for you. . . .

The Organisation Society of which he was founder and president for five years gathered into its work the extremists of both sides and the societies are filled with Orangemen in the north and with United Irish Leaguers in the west, and no political or religious questions are ever raised in the industrial work which it is agreed can be carried on amicably. A few years ago Plunkett went to a northern meeting with Father Finlay to start a creamery. They were met by the Orange band with orange sashes and the Nationalist band with green sashes who gave them a hearty welcome, and by mutual agreement each side left out the more provocative items in their programme, 'Boyne Water' etc. etc. The Recess Committee was founded in the same spirit, and Nationalist M.Ps met with Unionists from Belfast at their meetings to take council on the economic condition of Ireland. The outcome of the I.A.O.S. and its work is about 600 socieites of farmers continually increasing. The outcome of the Recess Committee is the new Department of Agriculture and Technical Instruction. . . .

Edited by Alan Denison

THE BALLYGULLION CREAMERY SOCIETY LIMITED

The divided community of Ballygullion unfortunately succumbed to dissension between Orange and Green and after trying to start a Co-operative Creamery it was decided not to proceed but to start two such organizations, one each for the two parties.

So notices was sent out for a meetin' to wind up the Society, an' there was a powerful musther av both sides, for fear either of them might get an advantage over the other wan.

To keep clear av trouble it was to be held in the Market-house.

The night av the meetin' come; an' when I got into the room who should I see on the platform but Major Donaldson and Father Connolly. An' thin I begin to wondher what was on.

For the Major was too aisy goin' and kindly to mix himself up wi' party-work, an' Father Connolly was well known to be terrible down on it, too.

So a sort av a mutther begin to run through the meetin' that there was goin' to be an attempt to patch up the split.

Some was glad and not afraid to say it; but the most looked dour an' said nothin'; an' wee Billy and Tammas McGorrian kept movin' in and out among their frinds an' swearin' them to stand firm.

When the room was well filled, an' iverybody settled down, the Major gets on his feet.

'Ladies an' gentlemen,' sez he – the Major was always polite if it was only a thravellin' tinker he was spakin' to – 'Ladies an'

A West Ulster example of the smaller type of rural cooperative creamery, spreading rapidly at the end of the nineteenth century under the auspices of the Irish Agricultural Organisation Society, founded by Horace Plunkett.

Harvest supper, or 'churn', Toome, Co Antrim. The last sheaf is hanging over the table and the photographer, W.A. Green, is seated at the head of the table.

gentlemen, you know why we've met here to-night – to wind up the Ballygullion cramery Society. I wish windin' up meant that it would go on all the better; but, unfortunately, windin' up a society isn't like windin' up a clock. . . .

Thin Father Connolly comes forward an' looks roun' a minit or so before speakin'. . . .

'Men an' wimmin av Ballygullion,' sez Father Connolly – he was ay a plain-spoken wee man – 'we're met here to end up the United Cramery Society, and after that we're goin' to start two societies, I hear.

'The sinsible men av Ballygullion sees that it would be altogether absurd an' ridiculous for Catholics an' Protestants, Home Rulers an' Unionists, to work together in anything at all. As they say, the parties is altogether opposed in everything that's important.

'The wan keeps Patrick's Day for a holiday, and the other the Twelfth av July; the colours of the one is green, an' the colours of the other orange; the wan wants to send their Mimbers av Parliament to College Green, and the other to Westminster; an there are a lot more differences just as important as these.

'It's thrue,' goes on the Father, 'that some ignorant persons says that, after all, the two parties lives in the same counthry, undher the same sky, wi' the same sun shinin' on thim' an' the same rain wettin' thim; and that what's good for that counthry is good for both parties, an' what's bad for it is bad

for both; that they live side by side as neighbours, an' buy and sell among wan another, an' that nobody has iver seen that there was twinty-one shillin's in a Catholic pound, an' nineteen in a Protestant pound, or the other way about; an' that, although they go about it in different ways, they worship the same God, the God that made both av thim; but I needn't tell ye that these are only a few silly bodies, an' don' riprisint the opinion av the counthry.' . . .

'Now,' sez Father Connolly, 'after what I've said, I needn't tell ye that I'm av the opinion av the sinsible men, an' I think that by all manes we should have a Catholic cramery, and a Protestant wan.'

The Major sits up wi' a start, an' wan looks at the other all over the room.

'The only thing that bothers me,' sez the Father, goin' on an' takin' no notice, 'is the difficulty av doin' it. It's aisy enough to sort out the Catholic farmers from the Protestant; but what about the cattle?' sez he.

'If a man rears up a calf till it becomes a cow, there's no doubt that cow must be Nationalist or Orange. She couldn't help it, livin' in this counthry. Now what are you going to do when a Nationalist buys an Orange cow? Tammas McGorrian bought a cow from wee Billy there last month that Billy bred an' reared himself. Do ye mane to tell me that's a Nationalist cow? I tell ye what it is, boys,' sez the Father, wi' his eyes twinklin', 'wan can av that cow's milk in a

Nationalist cramery would turn the butther as yellow as the shutters av the Orange Hall.' . . .

'Now,' sez Father Connolly, 'afther all it's aisy enough in the case of Tammas's cow. There's no denyin' she's an Orange cow, an' either Tammas may go to the Orange cramery or give the cow back to Billy.'

Tammas sits up a bit at that.

'But, thin, there's a lot of mighty curious cases. There's my own wee Kerry. Iverybody knows I bred her myself; but, thin, there's no denyin' that her father – if that's the right way to spake av a bull – belonged to Major Donaldson here, an' was called "Prince of Orange". Now be the law a child follows its father in these matters, an' I'm bound be it to send the wee Kerry's milk to the Orange cramery, although I'll maintain she's as good a Nationalist as ever stepped – didn't she thramp down ivery Orange lily in Billy Black's garden only last Monday?

'So, boys, whin ye think the matther out, ye'll see it's no aisy matther this separatin' av Orange an' Green in the cramery. For if ye do it right – an' I'm for no half-measures – ye'll have to get the pedigree av ivery bull, cow, an' calf in the counthry, an' then ye'll be little further on, for there's a lot av bastes come in every year from Americay that's little better than haythin.

'But, if ye take my advice, those av ye that isn't sure av your cows'll just go on quietly together in the manetime, an' let thim that has got a rale thrue-blue baste av either persuasion just keep her milk to themselves, and skim it in the ould-fashioned way wi' a spoon.'

There was a good dale av sniggerin' whin the Father was spakin'; but ye should have heard the roar av a laugh there was whin he sat down. An' just as it was dyin' away, the Major rises up, wipin' his eyes:

'Boys,' sez he, 'if it's the will av the prisint company that the Ballygullion Cramery Society go on, will ye rise an' give three cheers for Father Pether Connolly?'

Ivery man, woman, an' child – Protestant and Catholic – was on their feet in a minit; an' if the Ballygullion Market-house roof didn't rise that night, it's safe till etarnity.

From that night on there was niver another word av windin' up or splittin' either. An' if iver ye come across a print av butther wi' a wreath of shamrocks an' orange-lilies on it, ye'll know it come from the Ballygullion Cramery Society, Limited.

Lynn Doyle

UNECONOMIC HOLDINGS

There are said to be some 200,000 'uneconomic holdings' in Ireland. Achill must contribute her share to this figure. It seems a ludicrous thing that people should run farms which do not pay any more than they should run shops which do not pay. There is a certain royalty of extravagance about it. Yet many Irish farmers could never make ends meet, were it not for the steady gifts of sons and daughters who have gone to America. Thousands of others, like the Achill people, regularly cross over to Great Britain and raid it for the gold and silver of subsistence.

Aran Island cattle being sent to market on the mainland.

RECEIPTS AND EXPENDITURE OF A FAMILY *in ordinary circumstances*, THE RECEIPTS BEING DERIVED FROM AGRICULTURE, FISHING AND HOME INDUSTRIES.

	Receipts				Expenditure			
Sale of heifer or bullock	£4	10	0	Rent	£2	0	0
Sale of five sheep	3	15	0	County cess	0	5	8
Sale of pig	3	10	0	Tea	5	17	0
Sale of eggs	2	4	4	Sugar	1	19	0
Sale of flannel or tweed	3	10	0	Meal	7	14	0
Sale of corn	0	15	0	Flour	1	17	6
Sale of fish	8	0	0	Clothing	6	8	6
Sale of knitting, etc.	1	0	0	Tobacco	2	7	8
				One young pig	0	15	0
				Implements	1	4	9
	£27	4	4		£30	9	1

Home produce consumed by the family is valued at from £5, 10s. to £10.

Robert Lynd

IRISH CO-OPERATION

Sir Horace referred to the reputation of his ancestors in a speech that he made not long ago, as follows:

'I was reared in one of those old castles of the Pale, almost under the shadow of the Hill of Tara, where the Plunkett family for seven centuries have managed to cling to the same house. Of course, in the good old days, we fought for what we considered our rights, which was to treat the inhabitants of the country as mere Irish and to avail ourselves of their long-horned cattle without payment. I have never started a new creamery without a sense of restitution for their little irregularities. An old chronicle we have in the family runs thus: 'There be in Meath two Lords Plunkett, a Lord of Killeen and a Lord of Dunsany, and so it comes to pass that whoever can escape being robbed at Dunsany will be robbed at Killeen – and whoever can escape being robbed at Killeen will be robbed at Dunsany.' This shows that our family took an interest in the tourist traffic in those days, though our methods of developing it, judged by the polite standards of to-day, may appear somewhat crude. You will notice also the germ of the co-operative idea.'

R.A. Anderson, the permanent secretary of the Agricultural Organization Society from the beginning, told me the story as follows:

Sheep-marking in hill country. Robert Lloyd Praeger, author and naturalist, is standing in the centre background.

'An adequate staff was first employed who went about among the farmers holding meetings, delivering lectures, talking with them privately, explaining the advantages of education and co-operation, and organizing local societies in every county and district to co-operate with the general society in Dublin. This work has been going on ever since until we have now about ninety thousand members, mostly small landowners and farmers, although in the southern counties we have several prominent ones.

'The next step was to organize co-operative creameries, the farmers contributing the capital and sharing the returns . . . . They deliver their milk at the creameries every day and receive credit tickets for it, which are settled once a month. . . . We have now in operation three hundred and fifty co-operative creameries to which forty thousand farmers contribute. The butter is exported to England and Scotland by the managers under the supervision of a committee. The reputation of Irish butter has been restored. . . .

'Our next step was to organize societies among the farmers for the co-operative purchase of supplies of various kinds, for the purchase of seeds, manures, feeding stuffs, machinery, implements, carts, harness, and everything a farmer needs but his live stock. We have one central agency at Dublin acting for about two hundred local societies in different parts of Ireland, representing about seventeen thousand families, who buy everything they want in that way at much lower prices than are charged by the local dealers. They are always sure of getting wholesale prices, the best quality of articles, and there is no possibility of being swindled. . . .

'The next step,' continued Mr Anderson, 'was to organize co-operative credit societies from which farmers who are members may borrow money at low rates and keep out of the hands of the "gombeen men" – the Celtic word for usurer – who bleed their clients in a merciless manner. The loans are made for productive purposes only – to buy better machinery, more cattle, sheep, swine, and horses, seeds and manures, and other things of tangible value. . . . There are 270 of these Agricultural Co-operative Credit Societies in Ireland under the supervision of our organization with about 20,100 members. . . .

'There are various other co-operative societies,' continued Mr Anderson. 'Last year we organized thirty-two new co-operative credit societies, twenty-two co-operative purchasing societies, twelve co-operative creameries, five flax societies to encourage the cultivation and handling of flax, and six co-operative bacon-curing factories, where farmers can send their hogs to be slaughtered and cured in a proper manner, which enables them to get a quick sale and a higher price for their pork. We also organized a large number of co-operative poultry societies to promote the raising of hens and chickens, the shipment and sale of eggs and poultry, so that the farmers can get better prices, have reliable selling agencies, lower freight rates, and sure collections. Eggs are sold here by weight instead of by the dozen, so that people who raise large eggs have the advantage. The eggs are all test, graded, and packed according to the continental system. . . .

'The latest attempt of the Irish Agricultural Organization Society is to introduce co-operation among the small farmers who have recently come into the ownership of their lands to

Unloading a cart of eggs (700 dozen) at the market in Cookstown, Co Tyrone.

Basket-weaving on the shores of Lough Neagh, Co Antrim.

assist each other in building more comfortable homes for themselves and better buildings for their cattle and the storage of their crops. This is in the line of self-help and mutual aid among neighbors and furnishes employment for many days during the winter season which otherwise would be spent in idleness.

William Eleroy Curtis

APOLOGY

GENTLEMEN, – We, the undersigned, hereby apologise and express our sincere regret for having supplied to the Guardians of the Stoke-upon-Trent Union, in fulfilment of a contract for 'First Corks' Butter, a quantity of Butter in firkins marked on the lids thereof 'First Corks', though the Butter in question was not obtained by us from the Cork Butter Market. We deeply regret that we should have made use of marks purporting to be those of the Cork Butter Market Trustees. We undertake that this shall not occur again, and in giving this apology we desire to express to the Cork Butter Market Trustees our gratitude that they have accepted it, and refrained from instituting against us such legal proceedings as might be advised. We undertake to pay the costs of the publication of this apology, and all legal charges and other expenses incurred by the Trustees in relation to the matter.

Dated this 24th day of June, 1904.

RAWLINS BROS.,
Stoke-upon-Trent

Witness–
    FRANK COLLIS, Solicitor,
        Sutherland Chambers, Stoke-upon-Trent
To–
    Messrs. F.O.S. LEAK & PRATT, Solicitors, Manchester.
        Agents for Messrs. J.C. & A. BLAKE, Cork,
            Solicitors for the Cork Butter Market Trustees.

Butter Museum, Cork

THE BLEACHING FIELDS

We are looking across what looks something like a field covered with snow; an odd enough sight for midsummer. But the snow is really snow-white damask, laid out to bleach, on the borders of the ancient town of Lisburn, less than ten miles from Belfast. We watch the men bundling the long strips of white linen out of the carts, slowly unrolling them, laying them side by side on the grass, and so leaving them, to give the sun a chance to perfect the process of bleaching.

Having become interested in the nearly finished product, we begin to make enquiries of the earlier stages. We learn that the flax, sowed in well-tilled land, grows to be some

A Co Antrim bleach green, for preparing linen. Linen was Ireland's most important manufacturing industry during the eighteenth and nineteenth centuries, heavily concentrated in Ulster. Based on local flax cultivation, it grew to require flax from Belgium and Russia, and its many processes, from raw material to finished product, formed a vital part of the Ulster economy and of its rural landscape.

two-feet-six or three feet high, that little blue flowers open at the end of the long, slender stalks, that the petals finally fall, leaving a round seed at the end, half the diameter of a pea. Meanwhile the stem, which was green before, has become bright yellow, and then brown, and is somewhat crisp and dry. When this stage is reached, the farmer calls his workers, men, women and children, and hies him to the field. Then begins the pulling of the flax, which is pulled up by the roots in handfuls, to save the full length of the thread. Then, tied in bundles like thin sheaves, the flax is carried to tanks dug in the earth, and full of water; 'lint-holes' as they call them in the east of Ulster, using the Scotch name 'lint' instead of flax. Neatly laid in the water, the bundles of flax are kept down by stones; and there they remain for many days, until the shell of the stalk is thoroughly soaked and rotted. Along the outside of the shell run the threads of flax, and we shall presently see how they are separated. But next in order comes the drying. The bundles of soaked flax are taken out of the water, and spread in the fields, drying under the summer sun. It is a moot question whether the strong odor which arises from the rotted stems is, or is not, beneficial to the health of man. The flax water is certainly detrimental to the welfare of trout, and I can testify that, finding its way in some quantity into a lake, it makes highly perfumed bathing. But we must leave the question to experts to decide.

When the flax is dried, the stem is a dark brown, almost chocolate color, and quite brittle, where it was elastic and tough before. It is stacked on carts, and taken to the 'scutch-mills', of old turned by picturesque mill-wheels fed from lily-decked dams, but now often driven by prosaic gas-engines. Whirring wheels catch the fibre and crackle off the stiff stem, leaving in the hands of the 'scutcher' a handful of soft, pleasant-smelling tow, linen-threads in their raw state. Then, by various processes, some of which we shall see, the threads are separated, spun, woven, and finally bleached, as we see them now, in the fields outside Lisburn.

Charles Johnston

RURAL IRELAND – THE REAL STORY

The census of 1901 gives some interesting statistics as to the occupations of the Irish people. Of the 4,458,775, given as the total population, 131,035 were classed as 'professional'; 255,144 as 'domestic'; 83,173 as 'commercial'; 936,759 as 'agricultural'; 656,410 as 'industrial'; and 2,494,958 as 'non-productive and indefinite'; The inclusion of considerably more than one-half of the total population of the country in the class of non-productives tells in no uncertain way the real story of rural Ireland. It is this aimlessness in affairs which has within recent years been furnishing material for so much discussion and agitation for reform on the part of the publicists and government experts.

Plummer F. Jones

MARKET DAY AT BALLAGHADEREEN

. . . Ballaghadereen, a town near the border, is an uneasy group of public-houses and small shops, attracting broken lines of donkey-carts, loaded to the crib, along the surrounding roads. I passed through it on a market day. Donkeys poured into it as thick as wasps in midsummer. Men, gaunt and bearded, sat in the carts with staves, and were kings among the parcels of women-folk, who sat with their backs to the family ass, nodding and blethering under the pride of black bonnets. I met the disordered army of them coming down the uneven road that cuts the De Freyne estate in two like a crooked knife. They had moved from their cabins, poor and warped, but bent upon the enjoyments of a market day – upon gossip and whisky and small purchases. They had stolen a petty living from the jaws of a bog. They had driven the red heather from a few square yards of moor, and drained off the floods, and were now about to snatch the flying joy of a market day from under the nose of a black and dismal destiny.

Robert Lynd

GOING FOR A SONG

They had the ordinary fair in Clones every month and then there was what they called the middle-market every fortnight. This always happened on a Thursday – the fair-day and the middle-markets. There wasn't any cattle brought out to the middle-market. There was pigs and small calves, what they called *drop-calves* sold on the Diamond, and potatoes and oats and hay and everything else was sold on it, in the middle-market. But there was no large cattle or springers . . . .

I remember a long time ago I went to Clones with my father in a pony and cart, and at that time when they had their marketing done there was always ballad singers on the Diamond. They sung lots of songs and they told you before it what the song was. And there was a wee boy would go about with a great lot of them in his hand and he would sell to the people round about. They were priced from about twopence to threepence apiece and I remember they used to get them all sold, every one of them. Nearly everyone bought a *ballad*.

★ ★ ★ ★ ★

Oh you brave Irish people, wherever you be,
I pray stand a moment and listen to me.
Your sons and brave daughters are now going away,
And thousands are sailing to America.

Chorus

Ah good luck to them now, and safe may they land,
They are pushing their way to a far distant strand,
For here in old Ireland no longer can stay,
For thousands are sailing to America.

Oh the night before leaving they're bidding goodbye;
And it's early next morning their hearts give a sigh.
They will kiss their dear mothers and then they will say,
'Goodbye father dear I'm now going away.'

The 'Cockle' man with his donkey, cart and baskets of cockles, chatting at the roadside in rural Co Down.

Oh their friends and relations and neighbours also
They're packing their trunks now ready to go,
When the tears from their eyes it run down like the rain,
And the horses were prancing going off for the train.

It is now you will hear that very last cry,
And a handkerchief waving and bidding goodbye.
The old men tells them be sure 'til write
And watches the train till she goes out of sight.

It is God help the mother that rears up a child,
It is now for the father he labours and toils.
He tries to support them he works night and day
And when they are reared sure they will go away.

Robin Morton

FLEECED!

Pig jobbers regularly lay out the market and fix prices, and while the farmer knows he is being fleeced he has no remedy. In Ulster, where pigs are killed before the fair, they must be sold somehow. 'The dead must be buried,' as their saying is, and elsewhere where they are sold alive the farmer hesitates to bring the animals back and be at the expense of further feeding, when he is not sure that the next fair will not see the same gang at work and perhaps with a lower price fixed.

Flax sales are dominated in the same way. The buyers form a ring in the morning and fiat their ultimatums. Corn and barley are sold by sample, and the producers nearly always being fleeced on the excuse that bulk is not equal to sample. If prices go up he may be paid in full, but if they go down it is generally found that the sample was very misleading.

. . . I have made these brief sketches of their methods because I want to show how impossible it is for the unorganized small farmer to retain any fair proportion of the wealth he creates while forces which he cannot control take possession of his industry and exploit it. I wish to show how impossible it is to build up a rural civilisation while these loose and wasteful business methods prevail. While this goes on stagnation or decadence must continue. The farmer will economise more in labour, he will revert to the cheapest and lowest forms of farming, and labour will desert the country.

George Russell (AE)

ABUSES OF THE SYSTEM

I find it difficult to write calmly of the abuses of the credit system which once prevailed all over Ireland, and which still prevail in many districts, but especially in the west. Nothing is easier for the farmer than to run into debt at one of these country shops. He is invited to help himself to everything the shop contains up to certain well-defined limit. He may be

Market day in Dundalk, Co Louth, in the early 1900s.

Provincial Bank of Ireland, Hill Street, Newry, Co Down.

allowed a year or a year-and-a-half to be behindhand with his payments. The aim is to let him sink into debt, not so deeply as to imperil the security the trader has, but deeply enough to make it difficult or impossible for the customer to quickly extricate himself. In fact the idea is to have tied customers – men who must buy where they already owe money, who are not in a position to quarrel with prices or the quality of the goods supplied. When the trader has double functions as middleman, not only supplying requirements but accepting produce, the system is one of the most effective means of fleecing the farmer at both ends of his business which could be devised. A large number of rural traders not only sell to their customers but also buy cattle, swine, butter, eggs, oats, potatoes, and other forms of farm produce from them. Barter takes the place of cash transactions. In congested districts this system is responsible for half of the poverty. I made minute enquiries in Connemara a few years ago. I compared the prices charged there with the prices charged for goods of the same quality in Galway town. I found out what allowances in goods were made for produce bartered, and came to the conclusion that for every shilling's worth of produce the small congested farmer had to dispose of he received less than half its value. In the maps of ancient Ireland we see pictures of famous chiefs standing over their territories – MacSwineys of the Battle Axes and their peers. In maps of modern congested Ireland pictured in the same way we should find swollen gombeen men straddling right across whole parishes, sucking up like a sponge all the wealth in the district, ruling everything, presiding over county councils, rural councils, boards of guardians, and placing their relatives in every position which their public functions allow them to interfere with.

George Russell (AE)

BANKS IN IRELAND

	1850	1860	1870		1880		1890		1900		1910	
	Offices open	Offices open	Head Office and Branches open	Sub-Branches and Agencies open	Head Office and Branches open	Sub-Branches and Agencies open	Head Office and Branches open	Sub-Branches and Agencies open	Head Office and Branches open	Sub-Branches and Agencies open	Head Office and Branches open	Sub-Branches and Agencies open
Bank of Ireland	24	27	37	2	58	2	59	1	61	7	70	26
Belfast Banking Co.	21	24	33	–	37	–	38	22	45	26	47	30
Hibernian Bank	5	4	17	2	39	12	37	16	42	27	47	32
Munster and Leinster	–	–	30★	6★	44★	4★	38	12	44	12	54	26
National Bank	48	50	55	–	83	27	85	9	87	12	90	29
Northern Banking Co.	12	13	33	9	48	19	49	32	53	40	60	41
Provincial Bank	38	42	44	–	47	–	51	4	52	12	55	30
Royal Bank	1	1	5	–	6	–	8	–	8	–	9	3
Ulster Bank	16	19	31	–	53	–	56	52	64	69	73	87
Tipperary Joint Stock Bank†	9	–	–	–	–	–	–	–	–	–	–	–
			285	19	415	64	421	148	456	205	505	304
Total	174	180	304		479		569		661		809	

★ *These figures refer to the Munster Bank, which was established in 1864, and in 1885 was replaced by the Munster and Leinster Bank.*
† *Ceased operations in the year 1856.*

F.G. Hall

A STOCKING TALE

Norah detailed how the wool was bought by her mother (they were too poor to have sheep of their own) for 1s. per pound, scoured, well greased; carded on wool-carders (two flat wooden squares with handles and with pliable wire bristles fixed in like the bristles of a hair brush); how a little tuft of the wool is brushed backwards and forwards between the carders until all unevenness and tangles are taken out; how the wool is then brushed into light, fleecy curls, about six inches in length, which are spun into yarn by the simple process of holding the end of the curl on the tip of the spindle; a few turns of the wheel fasten and commence a thread, which is drawn with the left hand as the right hand turns the wheel. As the spinner spins each length of yarn – she spins a few yards at a time – the thread is evened by drawing out any parts that may be thicker than the rest, then hardened by passing the length between the fingers while the wheel turns rapidly; this length is then wound on the spindle, and another curl of wool joined on by simply holding the two ends firmly for an instant while the twirling of the spindle joins and twists the two together. Most of the spinning is done during the winter nights, when the family gathers round the fire, a good spinner keeping a couple of carders hard at work, while the chat, the laugh, and the gossip go on as fast as the wheel. Some of the wheels are clock wheels, which tick where a certain length of thread – a cut, or skein – is on the spindle, when it is time to wind off, the spinner counting her work by so many 'cuts' spun. The thread is wound into large balls, which hang up in the kitchen until wanted for the weaver to make flannels or for the knitter to make socks, when it is scoured, bleached, and dyed by the women, who all understand the use of a variety of vegetable dyes, which, while giving very brilliant colours, are wholly free from the danger to health that so often exists in the chemical dyes used in manufactories. The stockings, knitted by the women in every spare moment of day or evening, are well known to tourists and sportsmen, and are highly prized for their warmth and durability.

Mary Banim

THE LACE SCHOOL

The same rule applies to the lace school which has been established by the government through the Congested Districts Board in the old building used by the Catholic church before the new one was erected. The government pays a teacher and advances the material. The girls get the price their lacework brings when sold in the shops of London or Dublin or at the Eccles Hotel here at Glengariff. Miss O'Donnell tells me that Mrs Duke, the wife of the manager of the hotel, is their best sales agent, and a stock of samples is always kept where the guests can see them. Fifty-one girls are now attending the school, and some of them walk seven miles and back every day. Father Harrington will not allow them to attend the lace school until after they are confirmed, and it is a great inducement to join the church because they are able to earn forty, fifty, and some of them sixty pounds a year, which secures them better clothes, better food, and some comforts for their families. Last year this little school sold nearly three thousand dollars' worth of lace, and the money was divided among fifty-one girls who made it.

William Eleroy Curtis

A group of women in Co Donegal carding and spinning wool in the open air.

A lace class at Ardara, Co Donegal. A rare interior view of the work of the Congested Districts Board, established in 1891 to encourage skills and employment in the remoter, poorer (mainly western) counties.

Kelp burning in the glens of Antrim. The ash from the seaweed contained iodine and other commercial substances used in, for example, glass and soap making.

THE KELP INDUSTRY

The people have taken advantage of this dry moment to begin the burning of the kelp, and all the islands are lying in a volume of grey smoke. There will not be a very large quantity this year, as the people are discouraged by the uncertainty of the market, and do not care to undertake the task of manufacture without a certainty of profit.

The work needed to form a ton of kelp is considerable. The seaweed is collected from the rocks after the storms of autumn and winter, dried on fine days, and then made up into a rick, where it is left till the beginning of June.

It is then burnt in low kilns on the shore, an affair that takes from twelve to twenty-four hours of continuous hard work, though I understand the people here do not manage well and spoil a portion of what they produce by burning it more than is required.

The kiln holds about two tons of molten kelp, and when full it is loosely covered with stones, and left to cool. In a few days the substance is as hard as the limestone, and has to be broken with crowbars before it can be placed in curaghs [sic] for transport to Kilronan, where it is tested to determine the amount of iodine in [sic] contained, and paid for accordingly. In former years good kelp would bring seven pounds a ton, now four pounds are not always reached.

In Aran even manufacture is of interest. The low flame-edged kiln, sending out dense clouds of creamy smoke, with a band of red and grey clothed workers moving in the haze, and usually some petticoated boys and women who come down with drink, forms a scene with as much variety and colour as any picture from the East.

John M. Synge

FAIR PLAY

'She says true,' interposed Padge King, 'landsfolk can't always understand why we are so bitter set against the trawlers. They think the sea in beside the land is the same that it is a hundred miles out – all deep, an' the fish all a fair take for large an' small craft. But it's no such thing. Here's how it is. Galway Bay is only like a shallow, sandy bottomed pond. Very well. Us, with our wide mesh nets, just caught the *fish* – the large, full-grown herrings of the season. The trawlers – there's eleven of 'em out there, their beams pointed at us like bayonets! – the trawlers come into the shallow seas, with nets of big and little meshes kept to the bottom of the bay with great bars that sweeps – sweeps along, and gathers up all before them – fish, old and young, and sand. Now, mind you, the sand is (or used to be) weighted with the spawn for the next year. But the trawl sweeps up *all*. Why, I have seen shoals of young fish poured – a dead stream – back again into the sea from the trawlers' nets: what should be a stream of silver for the poor fisherman next year an' the years to come, lost an' useless! An', then here's worse again. The Almighty gives great sense to all creatures for their own protection, and fish have a high sense of what is destruction to their kind. The trawl bars ever an' always

Ardglass, a small fishing village in Co Down, in the herring season.

disturbing the bottom of the bay, the herrings, that used to come in millions, soon began to desert it and turn elsewhere for shelter, so it comes that every way our small craft has little or no chance where the big boats of the wealthy company can sweep all before 'em. An' so it is that there's poverty now in the Claddagh. We ask only fair play. Let us have a matter of ten miles of our own bay – from Blackhead into Galway – free to our craft, and no trawler allowed inside that line. Let us have that for even five years, and see will the fish return to our coast. God knows the rest is wide enough for all – rich and poor!'

Mary Banim

OLD MARY

It was in winter I first saw old Mary. On a bitter day, when the streets were covered with half-frozen snow, I noticed an old woman trudging slowly and carefully down the middle of the steep street. She walked inside a wide barrel hoop, outside of which she carried two buckets of water. She wore a very short petticoat, a man's frieze coat, and a deep poke bonnet, and there was a peculiar air about the careful walk and the set forward of the head. Up and down the street she passed and re-passed so often that I saw she must be a public water-carrier.

'That is a very old woman to be earning her bread, and in such a wearisome way.'

Smiling woman in front of a small shop, Co Donegal. Poverty and cheerfulness were not incompatible.

'Yes, and besides being very old, she is quite blind, yet she supports herself as you see. I never remember our town without Mary, the blind water-carrier – Wexford would not be Wexford without her.'

And here in Selskar I found the old woman at home, ready and willing to tell the simple story of her uneventful life: making no wonder of the heroism with which, from an early age, she had worked on independently, alone in the world, and 'dark' – the Irish rarely use the word 'blind', but that most expressive word which at once brings before us the full terror of the sad affliction.

'I'm over seventy years, praises be to God,' the old woman said, 'an' never yet had to beg the bit I eat, nor what pays for an honest, decent lodging, where I'm well cared – that I don't deny – well cared these one-and-twenty year, an' where Mrs Kelly keeps me in the cleanest of clothes, for it would go to my heart but to be cleanly. I am dark all my days, and lost father an' mother when I was only a child; but a' most since I can remember I earned my living as well as them that sees the blessed sun. Ah! you should have seen all the buckets of water I'd carry of a day when I was young and hearty; not but I'm able for a good turn yet, only the trade has gone since the new-fangled waterworks and pipes into all the houses put the pump out of fashion. There was a time when I carried water for half the quality of the town, an' I'd thank you to see how I could take first place at the pump – I was well able to take my own part. Now it's only the poorer houses want water, but a few of the quality takes it for old times sake an' to keep me goin', for I'm that used to being independent, an' to goin' about in the air, an' to turning into the Chapel to rest before the Blessed Sacrament when my day's work is over, that if I went into the Poorhouse, as some wanted me to do, I'd run down at once and die in no time, in place of being hale an' hearty, as you see me – content an' happy. Sure it's too good to me God is.'

Mary Banim

A CARPENTER'S PREFERENCES

At one end of this yard was a shed full of wooden boards, wheels, planes, drills, awls, hammers, and all the paraphernalia of a carpenter. From the midst of these emerged Mr S., bald-headed, wearing a short apron. To him I explained the nature and use of my ashen rod, and after much considering, debating, and measuring we hit upon a way of mending it. Mr S. had been at work upon the wheel of a donkey-cart. He makes many such carts, and showed me one or two examples of the finished article. But the making of them is tough work and affords no great margin of profit.

'There is nothing like a house-fitting job to suit me,' said Mr S. 'There's more opportunity to suit your own ideas; and you'll do something different for every house you touch. And sure there's more profit in it. Not at all like these wheels, every one of which takes so much blood out of an old man's veins. And when all is done there's nothing but an old wheel to show for it.'

R.A. Scott-James

The 'Black Squad', who did particularly dirty and difficult work, pose under the damaged hull of P & O liner China *(299, 1896), back for repair after running ashore on the Red Sea island of Perim in March 1898, in Alexandra Graving Dock, Belfast.*

HARLAND AND WOLFF

We are looking, from the north, toward the stern of one of the great ocean liners, in the Queen's Island ship-building yard of Harland and Wolff. Their works cover eighty acres, and employ more than 8,000 men. Here were built such White Star liners as the *Majestic*, the *Teutonic*, and their big modern successors. Here are repaired the ships of the International Mercantile Marine, which contains the chief American lines. Here, too, were built such ships as the *Arcadia*, for the Australian service. The steamships which have been launched here plough the seven seas. Something like a tonnage of 50,000 tons here enters the water yearly, distributed over a dozen vessels, up to the hugest ocean grey-hounds.

The firm of Harland and Wolff did very much for the prosperity and well-being of Belfast; and the great northern capital rewarded the two founders of the firm with the highest civic and parliamentary honors.

The ship before us is a liner of large size, with twin screws, and is about ready for launching. The clang of the hammers on the hull is silent, and the painters have just completed their work. A vast deal remains to be done inside. There are the decks to complete, the engines to put in place, adjust and connect; the cabins and saloons to build and finish; the electric light to install, and the thousand-and-one small things that go to make up the fitting of a big steamer. And all this without taking account of the funnels, masts, rigging, and everything that appears above the decks.

The two founders of this, the greatest among several Belfast ship-building firms, were both new-comers to Belfast. Mr Harland was an Englishman; his partner a German. But they agreed in the qualities of energy and judgment, and both saw that Belfast Lough was admirably adapted to the work they had in view, and they had the energy and perseverence to turn their insight into accomplished fact. Honors and titles later indicated the extent of their success, and the great influence it has had on the town of their adoption. Their stalwart shipwrights, locally known as 'the Queen's Island Boys', are recognized as a vigorous political and social element, of distinctly orange coloring.

Charles Johnston

A WOMAN'S WORK

Now we see the 'roving' and wet spinning – all done by women. This work is exceedingly interesting to a looker-on, who watches with wonder the activity of eye and hand, the care and dexterity, with which the thousands of spindles are kept in such order. One girl will tend as many as twenty-four spindles, thus doing the work of forty-eight spinners of the olden times, as each spindle is said to produce double the quantity of yarn that could be spun at the old-fashioned wheel, and it is wonderful to see the rapid whirl of the bobbins of all sizes as the yarn, from the coarsest to the almost invisibly fine, is spun and

Workers leaving the Harland and Wolff yard at Queen's Island, Belfast, May 1911. About 14,000 worked there at that time, some of them on the Titanic, *seen in the background.*

The Architectural Drawing Office, Harland and Wolff shipyard, Belfast: naval architects at work, c. 1912.

Interior of a spinning mill, probably Sion Mills, Co Tyrone. The linen mills were established in 1835 by the Herdman Brothers and expanded and improved in subsequent years with workers housing, a school and cricket ground as features (see p. 75).

wound on to them. It is very interesting and very beautiful work, but at the same time one cannot help, especially in the wet spinning-room, thinking how painfully hard these young children, girls, and women must work that they may live and that the rich may wear fine linen. Here is an atmosphere so hot that it soon blanches the bright colour out of the rosiest cheek; so moist, from water flooding the floor and steam filling the air, that the operatives live in a perpetual Turkish bath. In this atmosphere are little children – half-timers they are called, because they only work for a certain portion of the day – these tend the spindles and earn 2s. 6d. and 3s. a week. How can little ones grow healthy in such air? How can young girls be strong, standing all day long in water, then going suddenly from the hot atmosphere out into the chill air of the streets? Yet, because of the liberty for their holidays and evenings, they prefer this weary work at low wages – 7s. 6d. per week – to domestic service, where they would have the comforts and protection of home so valuable to them, if they but knew how to appreciate them. Still, I was told that the Belfast factory girls are, as a whole, very good girls, and they are certainly very quiet in manner and respectable in appearance.

Mary Banim

Women 'flowering' linen outside a thatched cottage near Ballynahinch, Co Down.

Chapter 4

RECOVERING THE PAST

*A*s the Irish people during the nineteenth century became more conscious of themselves as a nation with distinct characteristics, interest in Gaelic culture grew and gathered momentum as historians, literary and language scholars and antiquarians all contributed to new knowledge and a sense of recovered Irishness. Standish O'Grady's History of Ireland (1878 and 1880) was prominent in pioneering this enthusiasm for the past. Even more influential were the folk tales and songs published by Douglas Hyde a decade later, works added to by the young W.B. Yeats, who drew upon Hyde's translations and who was further stimulated in the mid '90s by his contact with Lady Gregory and the opportunity she provided to steep himself in the traditions of the West of Ireland. A parallel enthusiasm in popular and creative arts led to much embellishment, with shamrocks and round towers and heroic figures from the legendary past, of buildings ranging from churches to public houses as well as of book design and illustration, and the manufacture of trinkets and ornaments incorporating such imagery. Very significantly, this was also expressed in a revival of Gaelic sports resulting in the founding in 1884 of the Gaelic Athletic Association.

In the cultural realm, scholars such as Father Eugene O'Growney, Douglas Hyde and Eoin MacNeill led the way, the latter two being instrumental in establishing the Gaelic League, for the promotion of Irish language and literature, in 1893.

These central activities were mirrored by a growing popular rediscovery of the antiquities of the countryside and in a range of amateur societies for the pursuit of geology, zoology, botany, archaeology and kindred subjects – societies such as the Belfast Naturalists' Field Club (founded 1863) and the Dublin Field Club (1885) that joined the Irish Field Clubs Union, one of whose aims was to promote outings and knowledge-gathering expeditions to sites near and far. Although non-political, the leading sporting and cultural societies attracted members of the secret Irish Republican Brotherhood, who eventually succeeded in harnessing them to the separatist cause.

The Anglo-Irish literary revival, in which Yeats, Synge, Edward Martyn and Lady Gregory were prominent, focused international attention on Ireland while at the same time causing clashes with the 'Irish Irelanders', who insisted that art, at this significant time, should be subordinated to the national cause.

Clonmacnoise, Co Offaly: a general site view of one of the great monastic centres of medieval Ireland. Second only to Armagh in learning but far superior in the wealth of its remains, the monastery was founded in the mid-sixth century by St Ciaran. It was raided thirty-five times by native and Viking alike, between 834 and 1163, and finally was destroyed by an English force in 1552.

ENTHUSIASTIC AMATEURS

But all the time I was fast learning geology and zoology and botany of another kind through the Belfast Naturalists' Field Club. . . . The Club had been founded in 1863; it was an association of enthusiastic amateurs, remarkably well versed in local geology and biology, eager to impart knowledge. . . .

. . . Foremost among them was that remarkable man S.A. Stewart, trunk-maker, botanist and geologist; then there were Wm. Swanston, linen manufacturer and geologist; F.J. Bigger, solicitor and archaeologist; Joseph Wright, grocer and specialist in the Foraminifera; Wm. Gray, Inspector under the Office of Works, and in science jack-of-all-trades; Charles Bulla, commercial traveller and palaeontologist; S.M. Malcolmson, physician and microscopist; Robert Bell, shipyard worker and geologist; R.J. Welch, photographer and fanatical crusader in the interests of Irish natural history; Canon Lett, botanist; W.J. Knowles, insurance agent and prehistorian; and others – men of all sorts brought together by a common interest. It is noteworthy that in those times no member of the staff of the future university took part in the work of this enthusiastic and democratic society; in that respect things are different nowadays. With this Field Club group, men who knew all there was to know about local birds and insects and flowers and rocks and fossils, I foraged all over Ulster and beyond, picking up the field lore that is not found in any book, but passes from hand to hand, and so from generation to generation.

When I left the north in 1893 I exchanged the Belfast Club and Ulster for the Dublin Club and Leinster, Connaught and Munster. The Dublin Field Club had been founded in 1885 by A.C. Haddon and others; and the same pleasant scientific camaraderie existed as in Belfast – though of a more professional kind. There was no need to mourn a change that brought one into contact with R.M. Barrington, R.F. Scharff, G.H. Carpenter, C.B. Moffat, G.A.J. Cole, W.J. Sollas, T. Johnson, A.C. Haddon, E.J. McWeeney, de Vismes Kane, Greenwood Pim, and later many more. The presence of a number of other scientific societies in Dublin never allowed of the Field Club there attaining the local importance long held by its elder sister in Belfast, but since its inception it has fulfilled a fruitful rôle in popularizing scientific study, and has proved a useful training-ground for young people who later pass on to the larger societies. Field Clubs were started, too, in the nineties in Limerick and Cork. We established a joint committee which arranged triennial meetings of a week's duration in Kerry, Cork, Galway, Sligo, Donegal, in which all the clubs as well as members of kindred societies across the channel took part; these

'Snail hunters' at Murlough Bay, Co Antrim, May 1897. The photographer, R.J. Welch, a keen member of the Conchological Society, is seated on the right, with fellow members from England (L.E. Adams, R. Standen, G.W. Chaster and J.R. Hardy) who had journeyed especially to explore Irish mollusca.

Belfast Naturalists' Field Club visit to Crebilly House, Nr Ballymena, home of John Dinsmore Esq., during an outing to Slemish Mountain and the valley of the Braid river, Co Antrim, 29 June 1907.

Irish Field Club Union landing at the pier, Inishmore, Aran Islands, off the coast of Co Galway, 15 July 1895.

New Grange, Co Meath: one of the outstanding neolithic burial chambers, or passage graves, found in the Boyne Valley, dating from c. 3000 BC.

were especially useful in promoting inter-club intimacy of a fruitful kind. The latest phase of Field Club activity has been the formation in several provincial centres in Ulster of similar societies, affiliated to the Belfast Club and drawing from it much of their inspiration. My own heavy debt of gratitude for help in former days has led me to be ever a strong supporter of the Field Club movements, and in spite of the many alternative facilities now available for the acquisition of a knowledge of natural history, I do not find that the usefulness of the Field Clubs has in any way diminished. Especially among the younger folk, whose lives tend in these days to be so dominated by cinemas, dancing and motoring, the little antidote offered by the Field Clubs, the 'back to the land' attitude which is theirs, is I think salutory. It certainly leads to a better understanding of our country, which is an asset of no small value.

Robert Lloyd Praeger

THE GRANDEST MAUSOLEUM

New Grange, overgrown with copse, . . . rises from the crest of the field to the right of the road, with four great standing stones erect like sentinels before it.

These stones, of which the largest is eight feet high above ground, and nearly twenty in girth, belonged to a circle of thirty-five, set at regular intervals about the cairn. The circumference of this circle would measure nearly a quarter of a mile. The cairn itself is, like that at Dowth, girdled by a confining curb of blocks, eight or ten feet long, laid lengthways; and on top of these is built a low wall of dry masonry. If the thing were merely a pile of loose stones we should wonder at the expense of labour: but it is more by far. Here we have, as we have not at Dowth, the true original entrance, which is rather above the level of the ground; and under it is placed a great stone, its outer face wholly covered with a rich and deep cut design: the oldest example, probably, of that spiral ornament which the Celtic race in Ireland was to develop so profusely. Over the entrance is another carved stone, like a lintel, wrought with a kind of gate pattern in relief.

The entrance itself consists of two upright blocks and one transverse leading into a passage more than twenty yards in length, which here also is formed by gigantic stones. In some places the superincumbent weight has listed them, and you must crawl now where formerly a tall man could walk; but as you reach the end, the supports are upright and you edge your way without difficulty until suddenly space is about you, and your candle shows vaguely the domed roof of a vault almost twenty feet high. Here again are three recesses, and in two of them large oval stone basins – receptacles for what was left of the dead. In a sense, no mausoleum could be grander. With all our appliances to-day, what expense of labour and skill would be required to construct here on the hill-brow such a tomb? to drag from the quarry those monstrous blocks, to set in position first the uprights, the long line of the passage, the circle for the walls of the chamber with inset recesses – every stone standing

Cromleac (Dolmen) at Ballymascanlon, Co Louth.

a man's height above the ground; and then, starting from the ground level, to lay flag on flag in a ring, each flag overlapping that below it, yet not so far but that it can support the next; until the ring, gradually narrowing, makes a dome inside and is closed by a single stone on top of all? Will anyone say how men with no instruments but levers and their muscles accomplished the task? There, however, it stands.

And inside, wreathing itself about this colossal architecture, is manifest the early decorative fancy, almost puerile in its task of carving laborious patches of ornament without any general decorative idea. Yet the designs are effective in themselves, good types for development, lozenge, chevron, and herring-bone or dog-tooth, but above and before all the coiled spiral.

Stephen Gwynne

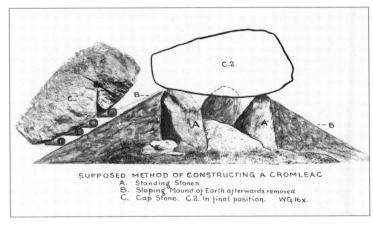

SUPPOSED METHOD OF CONSTRUCTING A CROMLEAC
A.   Standing Stones.
B.   Sloping Mound of Earth afterwards removed
C.   Cap Stone.   C.2. In final position.   WG.16x.

A diagram showing a possible way of constructing a Cromleac (Dolmen).

ANCIENT TRIBES AND GREAT DIVINITIES

. . . A woman appeared with candles and matches in her hand.

But why should we light candles in broad daylight? There isn't a cloud in the sky.

He told me to buy a candle and a box of matches and follow him across the stile, which I did, and down a field until we came to a hole in the ground, and in the hole was a ladder. He descended into it and, fearing to show the white feather, I stepped down after him. At twenty feet from the surface he went on his hands and knees and began to crawl through a passage narrow as a burrow. I crawled behind him, and after crawling for some yards, found myself in a small chamber about ten feet in height and ten in width. A short passage connected it with a larger chamber, perhaps twenty feet in width and height, and built of great unhewn stones leaned together, each stone jutting a little in front of the other till they almost met, a large flat stone covering in the vault. And it was here, I said, that the ancient tribes came to do honour to the great divinities − tribes, but not savage tribes, for these stones were placed so that not one has changed its place though four thousand years have gone by. Look at this great hollowed stone. Maybe many a sacrificial rite has been performed in it. He did not answer this remark, and I regretted having made it, for it seemed to betray a belief that the Druids had indulged in blood sacrifice, and, to banish the thought from his mind, I asked him if he could read the strange designs scribbled upon the walls. The spot, he said, within the first circle is the earth, and the first circle is the sea; the second circle is the heavens, and the third circle the Infinite Lir, the God over all Gods, the great fate that surrounds mankind and Godkind. . . .

. . . On our left was the tumulus, a small hill overgrown with hazel and blackthorn-thickets, with here and there a young ash coming into leaf. On all sides great stones stood on end, or had fallen, and I would have stayed to examine the carvings or the scratches with which these were covered, but AE pointed to the entrance of the temple − a triangular opening no larger than a fox's or a badger's den; and at his bidding I went down on my hands and knees, remembering that we had not come to New-grange to investigate but to evoke.

We remained upwards of an hour in the tumulus, and no sign being vouchsafed to us that the Gods were listening, we began our crawl through the long, twisting burrow towards the daylight; and in dejected spirit, wondering at the cause of our failure, asking ourselves secretly why we had been ignored, we climbed over the hill, to discover a robin singing in a blackthorn, the descendant, no doubt, of a robin that had seen the Druids.

George Moore

One of the three stone circles at Lough Gur, Co Limerick, where excavations have also uncovered many artefacts dating from the neolithic to the middle ages.

Muredath's Cross, Monasterboice, Co Louth. Of fifth-century origin, the monastery here lasted, it seems, only till the twelfth century. Biblical scenes are depicted on its two crosses (16 ft and 18 ft high), which are of very ancient origin. Here there are three carved scenes on the upright, plus the crucifixion at the centre of the cross.

PERFECT PEN-WORK

There are many manuscript volumes now preserved in Trinity College, Dublin, in the Royal Irish Academy, in the National Museum, Dublin, in the British museum and at Oxford. Perhaps the most famous of them all are the 'Book of Kells' and the 'Book of Armagh', both of which are in Trinity College. They are beautifully written, the former being a Latin Copy in vellum of the four Gospels, and the latter in Latin also, with considerable old Irish interspersed, also contains the four Gospels and the life of St Patrick, and a brief account in Latin by himself of his mission in Ireland. The Book of Armagh was completed A.D. 807.

Pen-work, of which these two books are beautiful specimens, was so perfect among the professional scribes of ancient Ireland as to deserve a place among the fine arts. Exquisite taste was displayed in design as well as in coloring, which is well preserved in these famous books even after the lapse of so many centuries. Metal work was brought to a high state of perfection in bronze, gold, silver and enamel, interesting specimens of which are preserved in the National Museum in Dublin.

The most noteworthy specimens of sculpture which remain are the Celtic crosses, forty-five of which are to be seen in various parts of Ireland. One of the most perfect of these is on Devenish Island in Lough Erne, and is of exquisite design and workmanship. Near the cross, stands the finest specimen of the round towers to be found in Ulster.

Daniel Lewis

Jerpoint Abbey, Knocktopher, Co Kilkenny. The extensive ruins of this Cistercian Abbey, built in 1162–5 and dissolved by King Henry VIII, attract the interest of a photographer.

Trinity College Dublin Library, home of the Book of Kells and many other early ecclesiastical manuscripts, increasingly subject to scholarly research. The architect was Thomas Burgh, and the library was opened in 1732, twenty years after the laying of its foundation stone.

Ruins of Cashel, Co Tipperary: a general view of St Patrick's rock from the North, showing the twelfth-century Cormac's chapel and the more ancient round tower. A royal seat from the fourth or fifth century, the ecclesiastical site dates from the beginning of the twelfth, when it became the centre of an archdiocese.

TINGED WITH SADNESS

The ancient Irish were lovers of music, and during the long period of their intellectual supremacy, instructors in music were often called from Ireland to England and continental countries. Many of the ballads which have been preserved are very beautiful, but nearly all tinged with a strain of sadness, as all the songs of a people must be when war, famine and pestilence are the constant concomitants of national evolution. The harp was the favorite musical instrument, and as we read of the great skill of the harpists, and the exquisite harmonies which they evoked, we are reminded of Thomas Moore's lines as to its origin:

The Origin of the Harp

'Tis believed that the Harp which I wake now for thee,
Was a siren of old, who sang under the sea;
And who often, at eve, through the bright waters roved,
To meet on the green shore a youth that she loved.

But she loved him in vain, for he left her to weep,
And in tears, all the night, her gold tresses to steep,
Till Heaven looked with pity on true love so warm,
And changed to the soft Harp the sea-maiden's form.

Still her bosom rose fair, still her cheeks smiled the same,
While her sea beauties gracefully formed the light frame;
And her hair, as, let loose, o'er her white arm it fell,
Was changed to bright chords uttering melody's spell.

Hence it came that this soft Harp so long hath been known
To mingle love's language with sorrow's sad tone;
Till thou didst divide them and teach the fond lay
To speak love when I'm near thee and grief when away.

To-day the harp and the minstrel have departed from Ireland like the Celtic language, the genius of which imparted to many of the old ballads the terseness of style for which they are remarkable.

Daniel Lewis

A FORCE MORE POTENT

Ireland has awakened to the fact that the songs of a nation are more powerful than the laws. The pen is mightier than the sword, and all the more so when the sword is unattainable.

The Irish people have discovered a force more potent than that of arms. A great movement is spreading over the land, a movement which has for its object the revival of the Irish language, the study of the ancient literature of Ireland, and consequently the fostering of the National sentiment. The Gaelic revival is one of the most important movements that has ever sprung up in Ireland. All over the country classes have been formed for the teaching of the Irish language. The children are learning it in school, and when they leave school they have special night classes after work hours to which they flock in hundreds with eagerness and delight.

In all directions people are speaking or trying to speak Gaelic. The names of the streets are in Gaelic. Many of the

The obelisk on the River Boyne, at Oldbridge, Co Meath. The obelisk commemorates the victory of William III over James II in 1690, a landmark in the Protestant domination of Ireland. Built in 1736, it was blown up by unknown persons on 31 May 1923.

newspapers publish a Gaelic column every day. The shop-keepers put their names over their windows in Gaelic. A medical man who can speak Gaelic will get an appointment before one who cannot do so.

Astute indeed were the minds of the men who first conceived the formation of the Gaelic movement – 'the Irish Renaissance' – as it has been called. Nothing has ever done so much towards crystallising the Irish National idea. I believe the promoters disclaim all political tendencies, and I am sure that many members of the Gaelic League fondly believe that they are enrolled in an association which is purely artistic and literary.

Never, so far as Ireland is concerned, has there been a stronger political force called into existence than the Gaelic League, I rejoice to say, is proving itself to be.

Home Rule is coming and nothing is calculated to assure and accelerate its arrival so undoubtedly as this wonderful organization which is at once firm, determined, attractively romantic, but subtle beyond description.

William Alexander Houston Collisson

AN IRISH NATION ON IRISH LINES

This lecture fired the language revival movement, marked the start of the Gaelic League and stimulated nationalist politics when delivered on 25 November 1892.

When we speak of 'The Necessity of De-Anglicising the Irish Nation', we mean it, not as a protest against imitating what is *best* in the English people, for that would be absurd, but rather to show the folly of neglecting what is Irish, and hastening to adopt, pell-mell, and indiscriminately, everything that is English, simply because it is English . . .

It has always been very curious to me how Irish sentiment sticks in this half-way house – how it continues to apparently hate the English, and at the same time continues to imitate them; how it continues to clamour for recognition as a distinct nationality, and at the same time throws away with both hands what would make it so. If Irishmen only went a little farther they would become good Englishmen in sentiment also. But – illogical as it appears – there seems not the slightest sign or probability of their taking that step. . . . It is just because there appears no earthly chance of their becoming good members of the Empire that I urge that they should not remain in the anomalous position they are in, but since they absolutely refuse to become the one thing, that they should become the other; cultivate what they have rejected, and build up an Irish nation on Irish lines.

. . . In conclusion, I would earnestly appeal to every one, whether Unionist or Nationalist, who wishes to see the Irish nation produce its best – and surely whatever our politics are we all wish that – to set his face against this constant running to England for our books, literature, music, games, fashions, and ideas. I appeal to every one whatever his politics – for this is no political matter – to do his best to help the Irish race to develop in future upon Irish lines, even at the risk of encouraging national aspirations, because upon Irish lines alone can the Irish race once more become what it was of yore – one of the most original, artistic, literary, and charming peoples of Europe.

Douglas Hyde

White Island, Lower Lough Erne, Co Fermanagh, showing a sculptured figure, one of eight found hidden in the wall of a ruined church and dating from between the eighth and twelfth centuries.

To Be Proud of the Past

By all means let the Irish preserve from the past what is worth preserving. Let their first care to be to save their own language from extinction – there are now no statutes against its use. Let it be no longer a sign of 'superior' education to be ignorant of the Gaelic, the sweet tongue their fathers spoke, the surest and strongest bulwark of nationality. Let them raise the necessary funds to complete the translation into English of the wealth of Celtic manuscripts that German scholars prize and too many Irishmen neglect. Let them continue to revive their national songs and dances. The ignorant belief that because a thing is Irish it must necessarily be 'low' will die of itself with the growth of wider knowledge.

H.B.

Oscar Wilde: An Obituary

A Reuter telegram from Paris states that OSCAR WILDE died there yesterday afternoon from meningitia. The melancholy end to a career which once promised so well is stated to have come in an obscure hotel of the Latin Quarter. Here the once brilliant man of letters was living, exiled from his country and from the society of his countrymen. The verdict that a jury passed upon his conduct at the Old Bailey in May, 1895, destroyed for ever his reputation, and condemned him to ignoble obscurity for the remainder of his days. When he had served his sentence of two years' imprisonment, he was broken in health as well as bankrupt in fame and fortune. Death has soon ended what must have been a life of wretchedness and unavailing regret. Wilde was the son of the late Sir William Wilde, an eminent Irish surgeon. His mother was a graceful writer, both in prose and verse. He had a brilliant career at Oxford, where he took a first-class both in classical moderations and in *Lit. Hum.*, and also won the Newdigate Prize for English verse for a poem on Ravenna. Even before he left the University in 1878 Wilde had become known as one of the most affected of the professors of the aesthetic craze and for several years it was as the typical aesthete that he kept himself before the notice of the public. At the same time he was a man of far greater originality and power of mind than many of the apostles of aestheticism. As his Oxford career showed, he had undoubted talents in many directions, talents which might have been brought to fruition had it not been for his craving after notoriety. He was known as a poet of graceful diction; as an essayist of wit and distinction; later on as a playwright of skill and subtle

Oscar Wilde: another face of Irish literary achievement.

humour. A novel of his, 'The Picture of Dorian Gray', attracted much attention, and his sayings passed from mouth to mouth as those of one of the professed wits of the age. When he became a dramatist his plays had all the characteristics of his conversation. His first piece, *Lady Windermere's Fan*, was produced in 1892. *A Woman of no Importance* followed in 1893. *An Ideal Husband* and *The Importance of Being Earnest* were both running at the time of their author's disappearance from English life. All these pieces had the same qualities – a paradoxical humour and a perverted outlook on life being the most prominent. They were packed with witty sayings, and the author's cleverness gave him at once a position in the dramatic world. The revelations of the criminal trial in 1895 naturally made them impossible for some years. Recently, however, one of them was revived, though not at a West-end theatre. After his release in 1897, Wilde published 'The Ballad of Reading Gaol', a poem of considerable but unequal power. He also appeared in print as a critic of our prison system, against the results of which he entered a passionate protest. For the last three years he has lived abroad. It is stated on the authority of the *Dublin Evening Mail* that he was recently received into the Roman Catholic Church. Mrs Oscar Wilde died not long ago, leaving two children.

The Times, 1 December 1900

MANY A FAMOUS MAN

From the time the College of Ulster was founded, many is the famous and enthusiastic Gael that spent days and nights in my house. There'd be a whole book in my litany if I was to name them all but it's proud I'll be till the day I die that, on my own floor, I shook hands with that noble soldier, Patrick Pearse. I well recall that autumn evening in 1906. . . . I saw this man standing looking at the serpent's rib over the gate. He walked over towards the house then. I knew nothing whatever about him at the time but after some talk, he told me who he was. As he left, I walked down the main road with him, step by step, and when we got to the top of the road, I thought he'd go down to the hotel but it so happened that he too was going to McDonnell's place. We moved on and at the bridge he stopped to bid me goodbye. I shook his hand and after saying farewell to him, I said: 'You'll come back to us next year?'

He was silent for a minute as he looked down the road.

'I'll come back again', he said, 'if it's the will of God.'

I never saw him again.

Many another famous man I met and many of them stayed with me here at Cashel. Among them were Roger Casement, that I mentioned before, Eoin MacNeill, Eamonn O'Toole, Robert MacAllister (who left no stone or hill unexamined), Seamus Delargy, the folklore expert, and our own Seamus Sharkey who came to us year after year. I had a great respect for everyone of them just as I had for all the scholars that came to us from Germany, Sweden, Norway and other countries in Europe. Most of them only stayed a short while

and so I didn't get to know them as well as I got to know some of our own people. . . .

Michael MacGowan

THE GREATEST FLOWERING OF LITERATURE

It was at the turn of the century, 1890–1910, that Ireland perhaps experienced the greatest flowering of literature. The inspiration of this movement was the Celtic past, but once again the pioneers – the playwrights, the poets – were of Anglo-Irish and Protestant stock. The movement started with the renewal of interest in the great Irish epics of the past by Standish O'Grady, the son of an Irish Protestant clergyman, and it was followed up by the foundation of the Abbey Theatre, with which almost all the Irish writers of the last generation were directly or indirectly associated. The biggest name, of course, was the great poet W.B. Yeats, like Shaw a Nobel Prize winner. Other names were Lady Gregory, J.M. Synge, Lennox Robinson, Edward Martyn, George Moore the novelist, and Bernard Shaw, who also wrote plays for the Abbey Theatre. *John Bull's Other Island*, which Shaw wrote about Ireland, was written for the Abbey and is, in my view, one of his very best plays. There were many writers. The whole history of this movement is described, in a rather caustic vein, in George Moore's brilliant trilogy of recollections, *Ave atque Vale*.

All these men and women were Irish pariots, and the movement they founded was immensely fruitful and productive.

Hubert Butler

JOHN M. SYNGE DISCOVERED

He was not a peasant as Yeats first supposed, but came, like all great writers, from the middle classes; his mother had a house in Kingstown which he avoided as much as possible, and it was in the Rue d'Arras that Yeats found him, *dans une chambre meublée* on the fifth floor. He was on his way back to Ireland, and might stay at Kingstown for a while, till his next quarter's allowance came in (he had but sixty pounds a year), but as soon as he got it he would be away to the West, to the Arran Islands. Yeats gasped; and it was the romance of living half one's life in the Latin Quarter and the other half in the Arran Islands that captured Yeats's imagination. He must have lent a willing ear to Synge's tale of an unpublished manuscript, a book which he had written about the Arran Islands; . . .

. . . Synge had gained the good-will of a certain tinker and his wife [in Co. Wicklow], and was learning their life and language as they strolled along the lanes, cadging and stealing as they went, squatting at eventide on the side of a dry ditch. Like a hare in a gap he listened, and when he had mastered every turn of their speech he left the tinker and turned into the hills, spending some weeks with a cottager, joining a little later another group of tinkers accompanied by a servant-girl who had suddenly wearied of scrubbing and mangling, boiling for pigs, cooking, and working dough, and making beds in the evening. It would be better, she had thought, to lie under the hedgerow; and in telling me of this girl, Synge seemed to be telling me his own story. He, too, disliked the regular life of his mother's house, and preferred to wander with the tinkers, and when tired of them to lie abed smoking with a peasant, and awake amid the smells of shag and potato-skins in the sieve in the corner of the room. In answer to an inquiry how the day passed in the cottage, he told me that after breakfast he scrambled over a low wall out of which grew a single hawthorn, and looked round for a place where he might loosen his strap, and when that job was done he kept on walking ahead thinking out the dialogue of his plays, modifying it at every stile after a gossip with some herdsman or pig-jobber, whomever he might meet, returning through the cold spring evening, when the stars shine brightly through the naked trees, licking his lips, appreciating the fine flavour of some drunkard's oath or blasphemy.

. . . And that same afternoon he said to me in Grafton Street: I would I were as sure of your future and of my own as I am of Synge's. Irishmen, he said, had written well before Synge, but they had written well by casting off Ireland; but Synge was the first man that Ireland had inspired; . . .

George Moore

AN EARNEST YOUNG WOMAN

Lady Gregory

Well she may say that the future will owe her something, and my thoughts moved back to the first time I saw her some twenty-five years ago. She was then a young woman, very earnest, who divided her hair in the middle and wore it smooth on either side of a broad and handsome brow. Her eyes were always full of questions, and her Protestant high-school air became her greatly and estranged me from her.

In her drawing-room were to be met men of assured reputation in literature and politics, and there was always the best reading of the time upon her tables. There was nothing,

A group of children of Inishmore, the main Aran island, Co Galway.

Inishmore: an exterior view of Dun Aengus, one of the great prehistoric monuments of Western Europe, situated on the edge of a sheer 300 ft cliff on this rocky island off Galway Bay. It was somewhat over restored in 1884, but not, it is believed, inaccurately.

however, in her conversation to suggest literary faculty, and it was a surprise to me to hear one day that she had written a pamphlet in defence of Arabi Pasha, an Egyptian rebel. Some years after she edited her husband's memoirs, and did the work well. So at core she must have been always literary, but early circumstances had not proved favourable to the development of her gift, and it languished till she met Yeats. He could not have been long at Coole before he began to draw her attention to the beauty of the literature that rises among the hills and bubbles irresponsibly, and set her going from cabin to cabin taking down stories, and encouraged her to learn the original language of the country, so that they might add to the Irish idiom which the peasant had already translated in English, making in this way a language for themselves.

Yeats could only acquire the idiom by the help of Lady Gregory, for although he loves the dialect and detests the defaced idiom which we speak in our streets and parlours, he has little aptitude to learn that of the boreen and the market-place. She put her aptitude at his service, and translated portions of *Cathleen ni Houlihan* into Kiltartan (Kiltartan is the village in which she collects the dialect); and she worked it into the revised version of the stories from *The Secret Rose*, published by the Dun Emer Press, and thinking how happy their lives must be at Coole, implicated in literary partnership, my heart went out towards her in a sudden sympathy. She has been wise all her life through, I said; she knew him to be her need at once, and she never hesitated . . .

George Moore

Statue of Cuchulainn, mythical hero of Ulster, and central figure of the Ulster Cycle Sagas, especially Tain Bó Cuailnge. *Sculpted in 1911–12 by Oliver Sheppard, it now resides in the General Post Office, O'Connell Street, Dublin.*

A round tower, altar and crosses on Tory Island, off the Co Donegal coast.

ALL THE WORLD'S A STAGE

The problem of Irish country life as stated by Irish dramatists has recently been a subject of discussion at the National Literary Society. The lecture which gave rise to the discussion is probably the last word in a worn controversy. The Irish dramatists are accused of misrepresenting the Irish country people. The whole discussion is due to a misunderstanding. All drama is an attempt to make startling combinations. It is obvious that the dramatist must take exceptional people for his chief characters. Again, the more powerful the mind of the dramatist the more individual will be his outlook on life. If one said to a sincere dramatist, 'In this country we have never seen the characters you portray', his answer might very well be, 'You will see them from this forward.' A dramatist makes national plays, not by expressing life in popular conceptions, but by giving intensity to the characters and the passions with which he is familiar.

Drama is often refreshed by a return to origins. But it is seldom that we have a dramatic mind of such simplicity as to go back to origins with sincerity. The Passion Play, arranged by Mr P.H. Pearse, and produced by the students of Saint Enda's and Saint Ita's Colleges, was made convincing by the simple sincerity of the composition and the reverence of the performance. No one who witnessed it had any doubt as to the fitness of the production. This Passion Play takes us back naturally to the origins of modern European drama. In a sense, it is the first serious theatre piece in Irish.

Editorial, *The Irish Review*, May 1911

Co Sligo: a carved stone surmounts a small cairn of rocks, one of many in the county.

Chapter 5

SPORT, ENTERTAINMENT
AND LEISURE

During the nineteenth century, urban living, railway transport, and labour regulation, which resulted in shorter working hours, increased leisure time and steady if small increases in disposable income, combined to encourage a growth in sporting organization, in participation and in spectating. The Victorian urge towards order was reflected in the formalizing of sporting rules and regulations and it was in the 1880s and '90s that association football, rugby union, hockey (for men and for women), were so regulated and their leagues and divisions worked out. In Ireland there was the added introduction of formalized Gaelic football and hurling, under the auspices of the Gaelic Athletic Association, initiated by Michael Cusack in 1884 and dominated from 1886 by Archbishop Croke of Cashel. Here was a conscious effort to counter the 'garrison' games of the British culture; a native attempt to draw young Irish people away from 'fantastic' imports such as croquet or cricket and attract them to traditional 'manly' pursuits.

The increasing involvement of the working classes in such sports did not limit their participation in the more traditional leisure activities. Ireland had and still did feature prominently among angling countries, while hunting, horse racing and shooting also remained popular. Now

golf was added and the tourist industry featured these sporting opportunities as well as myriad attractions such as sea bathing, sailing, tennis, bowls, cycling and the new motoring rallies. High and low culture filled the leisure time of the worker, the growing middle class and the tourist alike. The music hall and theatre became prominent, with pride of place going to the Irish Literary Theatre, founded by Yeats in Dublin in 1899 and known as the Abbey Theatre from 1904. Music abounded, from traditional folk dances and melodies to the pipe and flute bands of the North, and the classical concerts of Dublin, Belfast and Cork. Though there was political tension in the air and widespread poverty on the ground, there were distractions: whiskey and the ubiquitous Guinness were cheap; singing and story-telling and dancing cost nothing; religious festivals and secular celebrations were frequent and well supported. In higher echelons, Vice-regal levées, society balls, and military tattoos added to the cycle of enjoyment.

All these activities, old and new, gave employment to some and reconciled others to their otherwise mundane working lives. They attest to the rich variety of entertainment available during an era that was about to witness the cinema but which was still innocent of the television and computer age.

The egg and spoon race, a minor highlight of Strabane Sports, 1909.

Skating in winter during the 1890s, Co Armagh.

BY INVITATION ONLY

In those days linen merchants and their progeny scraped in along with the lower ranks of the gentry; hence our family party all wrapped up in woollen mufflers and gloves. There were, however, subtle distinctions in the manner of arrival. The aristocracy, wrapped in luxurious fur-lined rugs, arrived in shooting-brakes, victorias, ancient landaus, elegant broughams; in one instance, a jingling hansom cab. The rest of us rolled up wrapped in ordinary woollen rugs on hired jaunting-cars. At the gate-lodge I remember a ceremony of initiation, like being challenged by a sentry; a flashing of visiting cards, of invitations written on sumptuous notepaper, to be present on the ice. In those days there was no nonsense about the Common Man. The Common Man's place was back there at his work in the shadow of Belfast's belching factory chimneys, while the nobility, gentry, linen lords, linen merchants, *et hoc genus omne*, together with their sisters, and their cousins, and their aunts, disported themselves on or beside the frozen lake. In fact the gate-lodge keeper, looking extremely superior, like a man holding aloft an invisible flaming sword, shut the gates in the face of the Common Man and made no bones about it. No visiting card, no admission – and back where you belong! . . .

Hampers were opened, bottles produced, bonfires lit: all that was missing was a brass band playing the 'Skaters' Waltz', or a Hungarian string orchestra in blue hussar uniforms. Nevertheless, the inevitable couple who disrupt such occasions by skating better than everybody else were already

whirling on the ice. *He* wore riding breeches and had skates that turned the rest of us green with envy by curving back over his toecaps; *she* caused a lot of adverse comment and staring through lorgnettes by showing at least two inches of leg below the hem of her long, gracefully-billowing skirt. The general verdict among the lorgnette users in the victorias and landaus was that she was a foreigner – which, of course, explained everything, including the two inches of leg and the fact that she could do the outside-edge backwards.

The rest of us just clattered and stumbled round the ice, getting in the real skaters' way. The instruments (hardly to be classed as skates) on which I clattered were made of wood, with long straight blades inserted underneath. To put them on involved contortions with a gimlet (with which you bored holes in the heels of your boots) and struggles, reminiscent of the infant Hercules strangling the snakes, with complicated ligatures of straps. The snag was that you nearly always forgot the gimlet.

Denis Ireland

INFLATING ONE'S CHANCES?

Queen's Sports Day in 1889 turned out to be a sensational occasion. Billy Hume of the Cruisers Club won every cycle race which he entered by a long margin and there was considerable bad feeling when it was discovered that he was using a new device which many felt to be unfair. The new

Lining up for the start of the quarter mile cycle race at Portadown, Co Armagh, 1898.

Cycling for pleasure in the Dublin mountains, 1900.

invention was the pneumatic tyre and its inventor was John Dunlop, a Belfast vet from Joy Street, where many Queen's students had lodgings at the time. The original purpose of the invention was to save sick animals from distress while being transported by bicycle trailer.

Brian Walker and Alf McCreary

THE WAITING GAME

12 September 1909

The English upper classes are supposed to be very conventional. Everyone knows the old joke about pukka sahibs dressing for dinner when camping in the central African jungle. I came across one of this type in amusing circumstances the other day at Lahinch. Like all locals with a reasonably low handicap – mine is now 5 – I entered for the South of Ireland championship. Dad and Mother and Pat were staying at the Golf Links Hotel and I joined them there. The night before the championship began I was going along the corridor (wearing dinner jacket and boiled shirt like everyone else) when a voice called out – 'Waitah, bring me two w'iskeys and sodahs'. As there was no one else there except the man the voice was talking to, I twigged at once that it was addressing me, so said in a good Clare accent: 'To be sure I will, sir. Is it Irish or Scotch ye'll have?' Off I went to the bar and returned with the glasses, etc., on a tray. He paid and tipped me 3d. (I must keep the threepenny bit as a memento).

Well next morning being scheduled to play a Major So & So of some Londonish club at 10.5 I turned up at the first tee to see in my opponent the very man who had tipped me the night before. I thought he did not recognize me as he was affable enough though stiff; but having walloped me in the match by 5 and 4 and stood me a drink according to custom (the winner pays) he joined a friend and in a voice he probably did not mean to be audible to me he remarked: 'This is a damn queer countrah, wat, waitahs play goff heah.'

Edward MacLysaght

NORTH OF IRELAND CRICKET CLUB

MINUTE BOOK, OCTOBER 1900–MAY 1909

Note that during these years various other sporting activities took place on the ground of the NICC, namely football, tennis (Downshire Lawn Tennis Club tournaments), hockey, lacrosse, croquet, archery (Downshire Archers) and athletics (Queen's College), as well as band promenades.

Monday 29 July 1901

It was agreed that the application by Hudson Soap Co. for permission to have a captive baloon [sic] in the ground between 5 September and 28 September be left to the ground committee.

Golf at Ballycastle, Co Antrim: 'Bonamargie' green, looking towards the town. The modern game was introduced to Ireland in 1881 and grew quickly in the North, the first amateur championship taking place in 1893, the first professional tournament at Portrush, further along the Antrim coast, in 1895.

26 August 1901

Hudson Soap Coy – Agreement from same re taking ground from 5 to 28 Sept for Their Captive Balloon advertisement read and returned to them for certain alterations (free entrance of members, damage to grounds, balloon to be S.W. corner, and leave to put on a gate for matches) when returned with these additions, Mr Clarke empowered to sign agreement on behalf of the Club.

23 Sept 1901

Vice-Regal Letter – Letter from the Vice-Regal Lodge re getting a representative Irish team to go over to England next year and asking a representative from North to attend. Com'ᵉᵉ read.

North of Ireland Cricket Club

MATTERS (AND SKIRTS) ARISING

The Annual General Meeting of the Irish Ladies Hockey Union was held on 1 November 1899. Mrs Alice H. Strangways presiding. A motion concerning the selection committee was discussed. Then:

Various other proposals were made and negatived, one being that the selection committee should consist of not less than three members and not more than five members.

Another – that the International Skirts be compelled to be of regulation length, five inches from the ground, in order that the ball might not be so frequently lost to view as was at present the case.

At another AGM on 19 October 1902:

After prolonged discussion it was carried by a majority of two to one that players belonging to affiliated clubs be compelled to wear their skirts six inches off the ground all round. That the captain of each team be responsible for the enforcement of this rule, the infringement of which shall render the club liable to a fine of 2/6 for each offending member, to be paid to the Hon. Treas. ILHU and that complaint made by an opposing capt on the Hockey field shall be considered sufficient evidence of the infringement of this rule.

Minute Book, ILHU, 1894–1921

THE HURLERS OF DEATH

I knew a man – well did I know him – Pat Casey by name, from Clashmore below; an' that man, though he was dark in his manner an' didn't consort much with people, could work, by means of the knowledge he had, cures no doctor could understand the nature of. An' how? *Because he had served out seven years with the Hurlers of Death.* Oh! many's the one heard of an' seen them in the parishes around. Here's how it is. The Dead of

Cricket match, c. 1910, with Sion Mills in the background. The Herdman family, owners of the mills, encouraged recreation in their model factory village, thus contributing to the growth in company cricket teams in mill communities, such as, for example, at Comber, Waringstown and Donaghcloney (Co Down) and Muckamore (Co Antrim).

Tennis club, Co Cork, c. 1900. Tennis was then one of the most popular of games, relying heavily on private grass courts, but with a good number of town clubs also in existence.

Cove Hurling Club, c. 1908. Cove (now Cobh) was renamed Queenstown in honour of Victoria, whose visit to Ireland in 1849 began at that harbour town, but no self-respecting nationalist could play hurley under such a name!

one graveyard always play against the Dead of some other parish, meetin' by night, at the full of the moon, in one or other graveyard, an' takin' sides just like any other hurlers you'd see, only they must always have a livin' man out of their own parish to keep the goal; an' when a man gets the call, nothin' on the Livin' Lord's earth can hold him from goin'. It's an awful doom to be mixed up that way with the Dead, even in their diversions, an' few ever lives to see the seven years out; but them that does has ever after the gift of great knowledge – of all the 'erribs that grows, an' the sicknesses they cure, an' many a thing besides.

'My own mother (the Heavens be her bed! – Amin) seen with her own eyes the Dead Hurlers at it. She was comin' home late one night (a cousin of her own on the mother's side was wakin' three fields off, an' it wasn't so far but she said she'd slip home by herself) by the old graveyard of Ballysaggert, when, as she came along under the the ditch, she heard inside the greatest runnin' an' tusslin' an' fun an' diversion goin' on, as if all the parish was inside. So, to be sure, she up an' looked over the ditch, and there she saw the crowd of dead men in the height of the play – some she never saw before – some she knew well to be dead and gone many's the year; an' the stoutest player – he was fornint her in the moonlight, an' she marked him well – was the young man she left wakin' above in the house. But the strangest of all: there was Ned Hoolohan, own brother to the corpse, that the neighbours missed, an' said it was a shame he wasn't at the wake – he was keepin' the goal, his face whiter than if death was upon himself. He caught sight of her, and the terror that came over him she never forgot when he made signs to her to drop down – to drop down

before them that was around him saw her. The same man fell off an' died of the decline before the year was out.

'There's a graveyard beyond the boundaries of Tipperary, an' everyone knows that to this very time the hurlin' goes on there. What's more – the Dead leaves their hurleys in the ditch, an' no man alive dare lay a finger on one of 'em.

'Yes, I did, then, of a certainty know the power Pat Casey had, though he'd never speak to mortal man of what he seen in them seven years.'

Mary Banim

THE DISTINCTIVE GAMES OF IRELAND

The distinctive games of Ireland to-day are hurling and Gaelic football. Hurling is a game with some resemblance to hockey, and until recently it was popular in Protestant Ulster countryplaces as well as in other parts of Ireland. It is known there as 'cammon' or 'shinty', and I have myself played it with other boys with bits of sticks in a haggard. Hurling is a game played between teams of seventeen men a side, and one of the main differences between it and hockey is that the hurler is not forbidden to raise his stick higher than his shoulder or to hit with both sides of the stick. A hurler, however, will tell you that hurling is as different from hockey as night from afternoon. Besides goal-posts of ordinary width, there are two wider posts outside the others, and when the ball passes between these, a point is scored. Three points are equal to one

Canada/Ulster rugby teams pose in 1902. Sam Lee, to whom this photo was presented, is seen lurking in the back row, smoking a cigarette.

North of Ireland Rugby Football Club Ladies Committee, organisers of social and charitable events, 1908.

goal. The player is allowed to catch the ball in his hand, but is not allowed to lift it from the ground except on the point of his hurley. The game is rapid and vigorous, and is said to be more dangerous for the inexperienced than for the expert. It is being played more and more throughout the country every day, and there is no doubt that it deserves to be popular on its merits, apart from all question of national sentiment. Girls play a variety of hurling called camóguidheacht.

Irish athletes are not as a rule so positive regarding the merits of Gaelic football as they are regarding those of hurling. I have heard more than one of them declare that, though Gaelic football is a better game than association, it is not so good a game as rugby. It would be foolish for an unathletic person like myself to offer any dogmatic opinion on the matter, but I think Gaelic football could be mended into as good a game as any. It has been suggested at different times that it would be a more exciting game if points were abolished and only goals allowed to count in the score, for the point system exists here as in hurling. As it is, however, it is a fine game when played between two well-matched teams of seventeen a side. It may be described as a catch-and-kick game, for the player is allowed to catch the ball and to bounce it before kicking it, but not to hold it and run with it.

Gaelic football and hurling are played all over Munster and Leinster and in the Falls Road district of Belfast. But Connacht is a province in which, for some reason or other, the old Irish games do not flourish as they ought, though, of course, even here they are played in some places. Munster seems to have more

sporting vigour than any of the other provinces. In the industrial parts of Ulster, the working classes play association football to a great extent, and in nearly all the large towns through the country there are rugby clubs for the middle-classes. It must be said that the rugby game has been nationalised to a far greater degree than association, and it is claimed that the game as played in Ireland has various distinctions and virtues when contrasted with the rugby football of other countries.

Cricket has never aroused much interest in Ireland except within a comparatively narrow circle, and lacrosse, at which the counties of Antrim and Down excelled for a good number of years, seems now to be dying out of existence. Lacrosse, by the way, has always been played in Ireland as a summer game – not as a winter game, according to the English custom.

Polo is a favourite game with the wealthier classes, and grounds for racing, steeple-chasing and jumping are plentiful in many parts of the country. Irishmen are all supposed to be good judges of a horse. Certainly, a great proportion of country gentlemen, rich farmers and professional men are enthusiasts for riding and hunting, and the mettle of Irish riders and horses is proverbial.

Cock-fighting is still a favourite pastime in some of the midland counties of Ulster, and encounters between the cock-fighters and the police now and then form the subject of a newspaper paragraph.

Robert Lynd

Railways, and an increase in both leisure and disposable income, combined to facilitate excursions to such events as Race Day at Rosslare Strand, Co Wexford (see below).

The Strand, Rosslare, Co Wexford: a popular stopping point long before the line to Rosslare Port, to link with the new crossing to Fishguard (begun in 1902), was opened in 1906 (Fishguard and Rosslare Harbours Co).

Mermen: the camera never lies! These rare specimens have been captured on film by R.J. Welch at Lough Oughter, Co Cavan, during an outing by the Belfast Naturalists' Field Club.

Sand writing at Kinegar Strand, Bangor, Co Down, a popular seaside resort for rail day trippers from Belfast.

Fishing in the Silent Valley, Mourne Mountains, Co Down. Engineering work carried out between 1923 and 1933 dammed and flooded the valley, which now forms a principal reservoir for Belfast.

NATURALLY GOOD FISHING WATER

The natural advantages offered by Ireland to the salmon and trout angler are almost incomparable – quite so, if easy access and a moderate climate are taken into account. Compared with other parts of the United Kingdom the extent of naturally *good* fishing water is in far greater proportion than in England, Scotland, or Wales. Irish lakes and streams produce, as a rule, trout of far greater weight and of finer quality than those of the sister island; while Irish rivers are as favourable for salmon and sea trout as those of any country in the world. On the other hand, it must be confessed that in no other country have the angling resources suffered more grievously from mismanagement, excessive net-fishing, and river pollution. In the last-named respect, the general absence of manufactures might be supposed to save the fisheries from the lamentable devastation which has overtaken so many fair streams in northern England and Scotland; but this has been fully balanced by the effects of the pernicious habit of steeping flax, whereby hundreds of miles of admirable trout-fishing has been totally destroyed. When it is considered what enormous rents men are willing to pay for good fishing, surely it must be reckoned worthy the attention both of the legislature and of private owners to take measures for the restoration of such an abundant source of wealth. It has been known for long that good salmon angling would command plenty of customers; but the later refinements of trout-fishing, especially the use of the dry fly, have attracted great numbers

of people to a sport which fifty years ago nobody thought of paying for. Many of the Irish trout streams, if they got fair play and were protected from flax pollution, cross-lines, and other destructive practices, would produce trout superior to and more numerous than those of the southern English chalk streams. As a rule, these streams are admirably suited to dry fly fishing.

Some politicians may consider such a subject as too trivial for their attention; others may regard with indifference, or even with prejudice, anything that, in their view, would only serve to put money into the pockets of Irish landlords. But that would be only a small part of the effect of the restoration of Irish angling waters. Anglers must live as well as other people, and pay for their living. It is true that the owners of lakes and streams would benefit in the first instance, just as they have done in Scotland by the development of the sporting resources of that country. But the benefit does not stop with the landlords; it would be impossible to calculate to what extent the poorest districts in Scotland have been enriched by the presence, year after year, of wealthy strangers attracted thither by sport. One other consideration remains. Great Britain is a vast workshop, working at high pressure; the playgrounds are limited in extent, though the numbers of those for whom healthy recreation is indispensable are annually increasing. For one angler of thirty years ago there are it would be hard to say how many now. The advantage of restoring to Ireland the qualities she naturally possesses of entertaining anglers, would be a mutual boon to the two

The Kelvin Picture Palace, 17–18 College Square East, Belfast, 1912. One of the city's earliest cinemas, it was named after the scientist William Thomson, Lord Kelvin (1824–1907), who as a young boy lived close by.

countries; and the man, be he statesman or sportsman, who gives the movement a successful start, would deserve the gratitude of workers in the British hive, not less than of the struggling population of poor Ireland.

Herbert Maxwell

FAST (AND FEATHERED) FOOD?

Jimmy told us of an incident in duck shooting which only happens once in the lifetime of a chosen few. The scene was his cabin at the close of day – he was boiling something in a pot on the fire, when down the chimney came a whirring noise as of wild duck flying over. A glance up the wide and smoky aperture confirmed this, and, seizing his loaded gun, which stood close at hand, he fired, and was unexpectedly rewarded by seeing two plump ducks fall gracefully down the chimney into the boiling water.

And I suppose, said F.R.B., with an innocent face but a twinkle in his eye, 'I suppose that the flame of the fire sizzled their feathers off as they came down?'

'Indaad you're just roight there,' said our friend and mentor, and from the bows of the boat there came an incredulous chuckle, which Jimmy pretended not to hear.

Revd Charles Kent

WITH REGARD TO THEATRES . . .

With regard to theatres and so forth, it may be mentioned that the big towns have their theatres and music halls, but that, with the exception of the Abbey Theatre in Dublin, where Mr W.B. Yeats and his fellow-workers have inaugurated a beautiful and critical school of national drama, these are mere pieces of England unnaturally dumped down in Ireland and served for the most part by English touring companies. The Ulster Literary Theatre in Belfast is an institution, not a building; it has already produced several admirable comedies of Ulster life. Cork, too, has adventured successfully in the production of national drama, and in Galway – indeed, everywhere where there is a Gaelic League centre – companies have been brought together from time to time for the performance of short plays in the Irish language. The Gaelic League holds an annual festival – the Oireachtas – in Dublin, and in connection with this a number of prizes are awarded for plays in Irish, the winning plays being performed during Oireachtas week. As for the art of painting, the recently-founded Municipal Art Gallery in Dublin contains a collection of modern European masters – Monet, Manet, Degas, Mancini, Corot, and others – which is among the most important of its kind. Ireland, however, has a number of native artists of more than Irish reputation – Mr Nathaniel Hone, Mr George Russell (A.E.), Mr Orpen, and Mr Jack Yeats, to name no others.

Robert Lynd

A group relaxing at a forest picnic, probably in the Strabane area, c. 1910.

Armagh Dramatic Society poised to perform in 1911.

Bathing at Portrush, Co Antrim. Sea bathing became more popular in Ireland during the nineteenth century, especially after the railways brought resorts such as Portrush within reach.

PICKLED FOR POSTERITY

A photograph is only a piece of paper marked by chemicals, but we never think of it in that way – any more than we think of a human body as a collection of chemicals. We respect it as if it were an extension of personality, and almost regard any violence done to it as done to the subject himself.

Every photograph is unique,. It is not just a picture of a person, but a picture of a person that can never be again. It belongs to one particular moment of time, and to no other. The self of last year, of last week, is gone for ever, and we age from minute to minute. But when we are pickled in silver nitrate we live for ever.

So in one sense there is no such thing as an old photograph, for a photograph is the one thing that can never grow old.

Sprott Newspaper Collection

SUMMER CRUISING ON LOUGH NEAGH

By the Twin Screw Steamer, 'Lough Neagh Queen'

Commencing on Monday, 23rd May (weather and other circumstances permitting). The twin screw steamer, 'Lough Neagh Queen', will sail from LURGAN every MONDAY at 3.00 p.m., and from PORTADOWN every TUESDAY and FRIDAY at 2.30 p.m. for ANTRIM, arriving in time for the evening trains to Belfast, Larne, Portrush, and all stations on the Cookstown line. Circular tour tickets will be issued from Lurgan or Portadown to Antrim by steamer 'Lough Neagh Queen', Antrim to Belfast by the Midland (Northern Counties) Railway and Great Northern Railway, and from Belfast to Lurgan or Portadown by the Great Northern Railway or vice versa. Fares for the tour 3/6. Passengers can have about three hours in Belfast. Tickets will also be issued by the Great Northern Railway from Lurgan or Portadown to Antrim, and thence up Lough Neagh by steamer. Fares 3/6.

The 'Lough Neagh Queen' can be chartered by excursion parties on Saturdays and Sundays from any of the following places:- Antrim, Toomebridge, Portadown, Maghery Ferry or Moy to any port on Lough Neagh.

for terms apply to
R. M'Ghee, Manager Toomebridge

Sprott Newspaper Collection

SOCIAL EVENING IN YE ANCHOR CAFE

29 July 1902

The workers employed in Messrs. McCammon & Sprott's pork curing establishment were entertained by the members of the firm to a sumptuous repast in Ye Anchor Cafe on Wednesday

evening. After tea, Mr H.W. McCammon took the chair, on
the motion of Mr H. Wilson, seconded by Mr R. Jennings.
The chairman thanked those present for the honour they had
conferred on him by requesting him to preside on such an
occasion. He welcomed them all on behalf of Mr Sprott and
himself, and hoped they would all enjoy themselves. It was the
first time for them to meet in such a manner, but it was not
owing to lack of sympathy or friendly feeling towards them on
the part of Mr Sprott and himself that they hadn't met before
on an occasion of this sort; it was rather because it had not been
the custom of the firm to do so. One reason they had met there
that night was because they esteemed highly the services of
their employees. (Applause.) Another reason was the fact that
one of their workers (Mr Connor) had returned recently from
South Africa, where he had spent two and a half years fighting
for his King and country. (Applause.) An interesting programme
was contributed by Miss A. McCammon, Miss M.
McCammon, Miss Elsie Fergus, Blackwaterton; Miss Nora
Mulligan, Derry; Mrs Crozier, Messrs. Houston, Copeland,
Jennings, Wilson, Davison, Gardiner, Parke, McCullough, and
Neill. Grammaphone selections were given by Mr
McCullough, jun., which added greatly to the variety of the
entertainment. Votes of thanks were passed to the chairman,
performers, and Messrs. McCammon & Sprott, after which the
entertainment concluded by the singing of 'God Save the King.'

Sprott Newspaper Collection

PORTADOWN BOYS BRIGADE

Inspection of the Boys Brigade

The annual inspection of the First Portadown Company of
the Boys Brigade was held in the Lecture Hall on Friday
evening, the inspecting officer being Mr Thomas
Cottingham, D.I., R.I.C. The proceedings commenced
with the singing of a portion of the 100th Psalm, after
which Captain Mawhinney put the company through the
various exercises. The smart, soldierly bearing of the lads on
parade, their precision in marching, and the efficiency with
which they handled their rifles was much admired by all
present. It was evident that Captain Mawhinney had
devoted much time and attention to the training of the
boys, and their performance did him credit. The
programme was as follows:- Inspection, company drill and
exercise with arms, tug of war, dumb bells, high jump
handicap, figure marching, barbells, and drill down
competition.

During an interval in the programme, Rev. W.J. Macaulay,
B.A., chaplain, delivered a brief address, pointing out the
advantages of the training which the boys of the company
received. He thought that too much praise could not be
given to Captain Mawhinney for the trouble he had taken in
training the boys. He had devoted a great deal of time to the
work, and he had been eminently successful. (Applause.)

The Wilson and Duffy Combined Circus: this photograph of the entire company was taken probably at Strabane, Co Tyrone, c. 1911.

When the exercises had concluded, District-Inspector Cottingham said it gave him great pleasure to attend there on the occasion of the first annual inspection of the company. He was very much pleased with the smart, intelligent appearance the boys presented on parade. They were clean and tidy and well put on. They went through their drill and other movements in a manner that reflected great credit not only on themselves but on their instructor. The training the boys were now receiving would he had no doubt, cultivate and develop in them a spirit of manliness, courtesy, and self-respect – characteristics which would tell in no small degree to their advantage in after life. He would always be pleased to hear of the success of the boys of that company. They went through their drill remarkably well. He was particularly struck with the very fine manner in which they handled their arms, and their marching was excellent. (Applause.)

Sprott Newspaper Collection

EDITH SOMERVILLE AT THE MAXWELL DANCE

The dancing room was very well arranged – an *excellent* floor, and the Chips [chaperones] all sat in an inner room and watched the giddy scene through an immense open double door way. The music was a nice solid little professional pianiste from Cork, who played exceedingly well and didn't doldromise between the dances for hours, as all amateurs do. Harry had gone via the ferry and then in an inside car with Grace Pork and was there when we arrived. He was perfectly black with fury and came up to me saying 'The whole thing is a mistake – I'm going home'. When I asked why, he said that Swanton – who was making feverish efforts to show he wasn't hired to attend for the night – had come to him and said whenever he wasn't dancing he – S. – would be very glad to go upstairs and smoke with him!

Poor Harry – he presently trod a measure with Grace that soothed him; and he was not reduced to the necessity of huggermuggering with Mr Swanton as he danced like mad all the time. There were a good number of people there. The women being those whom you wot of – less the Bechers and the Girlies – but the men were mostly strangers. On the whole a much better lot than the D'Avigdor eggs. Mr Maxwell did the honours very well and nicely, and so did she, on the whole, though she was much occupied with a small bald barrister from Dublin called Manders. He looked a good dancer, but I was not introduced to him (nor indeed was anyone else: he was a patent.) Mrs Maxwell brought up one of the most odious looking bounders you ever saw and introduced him as 'My brother'. Strange to say – not being well up in the peerage – I didn't know his name. . . .

. . . Mrs Maxwell introduced me to a rather nice boy, a sub Inspector in the R.I.C., who had come from Skull for this dance! His name was Irwin, and he was a nice simple young creature and a foully bad dancer. He clasped his partner tightly to his breast and then stooped over so much that he pressed a burning and moist ear closely to her forehead. I could feel the mark of it during our infrequent pauses. He

Scouts assemble for healthy action in response to Baden Powell's call.

felt a solemn responsiblity on him to dance as much as possible, and fled round and round the room with heavy breathings, gasping 'thankyou' at the conclusion of each course. If Hildegarde tells you that she and Egerton saw me proposing to him you need not believe her. They sat out a few dances in order to invent the story — which really is not true, or even amusing. . . .

After two dances, running, with her, he asked me for a dance. I coldly assented but really he danced so well that my heart warmed to him, and when afterwards he asked me if I knew Lewis Morris's poetry 'Epic of Hades' etc I almost loved him. We thereupon sat out two dances, and I discovered most interesting things about his love of books, and poetry, and the musical glasses generally. He has read a great deal, in the most curious simple kind of way and knows a great deal more than he thinks — I then proceeded to dance two dances on end with him, and finally went into supper, by which time I had promised to lend him some of Howell's novels — Once I was very near making a great mistake. He asked if I had seen a critique upon the revival of an opera. I asked who it was by — he said 'he didn't quite know, but he thought the composer's name was Ross-in-I' 'Who' I said — 'Ross-in-I' then I knew, *Rossini!* It sounded like a service — Farrant in D. But I never said a word.

Edited by Gifford Lewis

Ladies playing billiards, c. 1910, at the Grehan family home, Clonmeen, Banteer, Co Cork.

Dancing at the cross roads: set dancing at Knockmonalea Cross, Youghal, Co Cork, in the early 1900s.

Chapter 6

MIND AND BODY: EDUCATION, HEALTH AND HOUSING

Condemned by Patrick Pearse as 'a murder machine', for its stultifying and brain-deadening lack of imagination, the educational system in Ireland a hundred years ago was inadequate. While the Irish language declined, literacy in English had improved through the primary structure and was widespread by the turn of the century, but a system designed to bring children of all denominations together had become largely separated with few Protestants and Catholics attending the same schools. Standards were low and attendance casual.

Intermediate schools, fee-charging apart from the Christian Brothers Schools that expanded in number throughout the century, were few and their standards generally poor. There had been some expansion, and some notable advances in the education of girls, although it was still too often concerned with manners rather than learning. Girls' schools included some exceptional establishments, among them Protestant Alexandra College, Dublin, and Victoria College, Belfast, and some Catholic colleges, run by religious orders such as the Dominicans. The 1879 Intermediate Act had belatedly introduced payment by results and new examinations and a common syllabus, but these encouraged rote learning and regurgitation.

At university level, the system seemed narrower still. In 1880 the Royal University was established as a degree-awarding body to serve the disparate colleges and other establishments willing to prepare their pupils for its degrees. However, the numbers attending remained pitifully small and this was to remain the case even after the University Act of 1908, referred to in the Introduction.

Early in the century it was recognized that responsibility for health care, as for education, was beyond local means and required government initiative. Thus, dispensaries were established from 1805, fever hospitals from 1814, and county medical officers appointed from 1819. Provision was gradually extended to cover the whole country, and included county lunatic asylums and the workhouse system. Begun in 1838, the latter provided another institution in which to deposit groups who were then considered to be the flotsam of society – the old, the disabled, the non-violent simple-minded, even unmarried mothers.

Housing standards also improved. Census returns indicate a gradual rise in two- to four-roomed homes and fewer one-roomed cabins, although here and there primitive sod dwellings and huts remained. One reason for this progress was the steady decline in population, the same resources having to cover a smaller number of houses. There was also a growing number of middle-class houses in cities, small towns and on more prosperous farms, again reflecting the overall improvement.

Fishermen's thatched cottages, Aird townland, near the Giant's Causeway, Co Antrim. The old lady in the linen cap is talking to tourists from Pittsburg. The big pot used for boiling potatoes is displayed with pride, standing against the cottage wall.

Staff and pupils pose at Cloughroe National School, north-west Ulster.

NEW SCHEMES

At the present time to be interested in education was the fashion. They might notice along the whole line of education, from the primary school to the university, changes taking place or threatened. In primary education the Commissioners had issued a new scheme. As a manager of some schools, he honestly confessed he did not understand the plan or the rules. He hoped the Commissioners themselves did. The scheme of Intermediate education had just come out of the repairing shop, let them hope, made more efficient for their usefulness. A new scheme of technical instruction was launched, and he expected great good from it, and a Royal Commission was sitting on university education. It required more knowledge than he possessed to say whether another 'chick', some new university, would be produced, or an addled egg remain as a reminder of the labour. It might be noted all those movements had been accompanied with much noise. Speeches without end, letters without number through the land, and they were all also financed and backed up with large grants from the public purse. But whilst all those movements had been taking place amongst much clamour, another movement just as important, perhaps more important and far reaching, had been taking place silently. He meant the higher education of women.

That movement, so far as he could see, had been carried on mainly by the individual effort of a few ladies who realised the great want in their old methods, and who, being blessed by God with a great genius for organization and ability of a very high order, used their gifts with the enthusiasm of apostles of a great movement in furthering the cause, and with great results and signal success such as the history of that College afforded, so much so that the objections so frequently heard twenty years ago were now silenced.

Revd Dr O. Loughlin

A NATIONAL SCHOOL

One day I knocked at the door of the pretty national schoolhouse on Bog Lane, and was pleasantly invited to enter. The room was perhaps forty feet long and twenty-five feet wide, its ceiling being the undecorated roof. The walls were whitewashed and well hung with maps and pictures illustrating natural history. The head-master's desk was in one corner, and there was a small fireplace near it. The boys sat at long deal desks. The room contained eighty-four pupils from three years of age to fifteen. The assistant was teaching at one side of the room, and two of the older boys were attending to other classes. Teachers of these national schools are divided into four grades, and are paid respectively $175, $220, $300, and $350 a year, but success in attaining certain results brings additional payment nearly doubling these sums. The government furnishes the text-books to the pupils at a trifling cost, the primer selling for a cent, and the fifth reader, the largest and highest of the series, for twelve cents. The schools have eight weeks vacation in the year, and any holiday is to be taken from this allowance.

The room was all talking and studying at once, but a clap of the master's hand would still it for a minute. Once in a while the master would say, 'Mike O'Keefe, be afther doing your business at once.' 'Jim, is that you a-blathering? And what about?' 'Indade, Pat, it's too bold ye are.' But with all its seeming crudeness to one accustomed to the martinet discipline of a New England school, there was an intelligence among the pupils that might have shamed their more methodical American contemporaries. Government positions of certain grades are filled by competitive examinations, and these boys spur themselves to outrank the privately educated sons of gentlemen.

Presently at the door appeared the gentle faces of the nuns who had come to give religious instruction, for the school is Catholic, and the priest controls the appointment of its teachers. 'There's a Protestant school in the village,' said the master, 'but whin the byes git big, they're after shying their cap at the misthress, if she be young, – and thin they come here.'

Albert LeRoy Bartlett

A GREAT WOMAN

I just want to leave with you an impression of that great woman, Dr Margaret Byers, as I remember her.

How did she appear to the schoolgirls of fifty years ago – at the end of Victoria's reign? Well, we knew something of what she had achieved, and we were proud of that. We knew that she had fought a tremendous fight, together with Miss Buss and Miss Beale, to secure educational advantages for girls equal to those of their brothers. As a result of their

Moy National School No. 2, on the Co Armagh–Tyrone border: the drawing class.

efforts we had on our Staff, as well as Oxford and Cambridge graduates, some of the very first women graduates in Ireland (you can see on the school walls a photograph of a group of them in wonderful Victorian dresses under their academic gowns).

Those were things which the public knew also – but what did we known directly, from our personal contact? I have heard Mrs Byers called awe-inspiring. I would rather say that she inspired great respect. She was dignified and commanding, but at the same time genial. From her portrait in the Lecture Hall you know what she looked like, I always think of her wearing, as she so often did, a wide black bonnet with an upstanding ostrich feather. We knew her to be just, and good and kind. Generous by instinct and by upbringing, she followed the scriptural injunction not to let her left hand know what her right hand did. In her County Down home she had been brought up strictly – even puritanically, but she was surprisingly broadminded for the times. By example even more than by precept she established in the school a tradition of public spiritedness and social service – the Victoria Homes for Destitute Little Girls, the Prison Gate Mission and the Damascus Mission for Girls bear witness

to this. This tradition I am happy to say has been upheld by successive generations of Victorians.

By giving us plenty of freedom and encouragement to run our own games and societies she provided us with a very useful training for after life. Queen Victoria recognised her pioneer work by commanding in her Jubilee Year that the name of the school should be changed to Victoria College.

Trinity College, Dublin, paid a great tribute to her by conferring on her the degree of LL.D. She was a great woman.

Speech by Mrs Faris, 1954

THE GUILD CONFERENCE

DEAR EDITOR, – Some of your readers may perhaps be interested to hear of the Guild Conference which took place in College on May 3rd. At it Lady Coote read a paper on 'Leisure', of which commodity we all felt that we possessed too little. Miss Ford's paper on 'The Tyranny of Convention' served to tear away the veil which hung over the cruelties perpetrated on the lower creation to enable us women to adorn ourselves

The gymnasium, Victoria College, Belfast: young ladies, too, combined learning with physical fitness.

according to our fancy. Mrs Tenant, well-known as an Inspector of Factories, spoke of the grave danger to the life of the nation consequent on the evils of factory life. Miss Paget's paper on 'Working Girls' Clubs' has stirred some members of the Guild to such an extent that they wish to form a Working Girls' Club in Dublin. A committee has been elected, and inquiries are being made as to the possibility of starting such a club, and the best way of conducting it. The account given of the tenement houses shows a distinct improvement in their condition. The rent is more regularly paid, the yards are better kept, and water has now been laid on up to the second storey. The dividend has been regularly paid to the shareholders.

The chief development in the work of the Guild has been the formation of the Social Service Union, and the foundation of Bursaries for women of gentle birth and education who, owing to ill-health or old age, are unable to maintain themselves.

A Games Club, the inaugural meeting of which took place on April 21st, has now susperseded the old Hockey and Tennis Club. We are now in possession of a permanent field, and we have cricket, croquet, basket-ball, and possibly lacrosse.

The various College Societies are flourishing, the Students' Union having taken a new lease of life. A new Society has been formed – a Temperance one – which already numbers over 100 members. . . .

J.R. Campbell
(Ed. *Alexandra College Magazine*)

SCHOOL ROUTINE

The whole school, which in its palmiest days touched about 200 pupils, assembled in the big schoolroom at the rere of the house on Rathmines road on the north side of Rathmines R.C. chapel, as the fine domed church was then known. Punctuality was not one of Benson's conspicuous virtues. He and the boarders had to walk over from the residence house at Elm Park, Ranelagh, and it was not always at ten o'clock precisely

Alexandra College, Earlsfort Terrace, Dublin, founded in 1866 and the principal school for ladies (Protestant) and another pioneer of female education. It was the religious orders, Ursuline, Presentation, Dominican, Loreto, the Sisters of Mercy and others, who led the way in female education for Catholic girls in Ireland.

that the party arrived at its destination. Meanwhile, the noise during those waiting minutes was unspeakable; tustles among the younger fry were being enjoyed, darts were flying, whistling and cat-calls were adding to the din. . . . on the left hand side of the big schoolroom beyond the stove, where was a raised desk, occupied by a junior Prefect. . . . On the opposite side of the room was a tall, thoughtful-looking, quiet, inconspicuous boy named G.W. Russell, afterwards to become a writer, poet, and artist whose well-known pen-name was 'Æ'.

From the cloak-room which was entered from the front hall a gentle descent led into the big school-room. On the slope the Captain and Prefects were drawn up awaiting the advent of the Governor, the appellation by which the Head was usually disignated. Suddenly a 'nix' passed from mouth to mouth, and from a *forte* by way of a gentle *diminuendo*, ending in complete silence, the uproar ceased and everyone stood to attention. To the strains of an opening voluntary on the organ a procession of gowned prefects proceeded up the room followed by the Captain and Headmaster, a momentary interruption being the reverent bow exchanged between the Head and James Robinson, the junior Prefect mentioned already, whose stall was on the ground floor. . . .

At the entrance to the platform which was reached by a short stair-way the procession divided and the Head walked through the bowing line of Prefects, followed in order by the Captain, the Senior Prefect, the Choir Prefect and the ordinary Prefects who took their respective places each side of the platform. . . .

T.W.E. Drury

A PASSIONATE ENTHUSIASM

Of late, too, we have had fine prospects opened out by the way in which important girls' schools like Alexandra College in Dublin – one of the principal Protestant schools in the country – have shown an inclination to play a significant part in the life of Ireland. Add to this the fact that last year a Catholic boys' school, St Enda's, was opened in Dublin as an institution intended to be as Irish as Eton or the City of London School is English.

St Enda's, comfortably set in a beautiful garden, is the fruit of a passionate enthusiasm. It is an effort to accomplish the dream of the headmaster, Mr P.H. Pearse, a barrister, a scholar, and the editor of *An Claidheamh Soluis*, the official journal of the Gealic League. In the hall as one enters one is faced by a lunette representing Cuchullain at the heroic feats of his boyhood. In another room are pictures by Mr George Russell (A.E.), Mr Jack Yeats, and others. High on the walls of the principal class-room is a line of the names of the great heroes of Ireland, coming down to Wolfe Tone and Robert Emmet and Thomas Davis. The teaching is carried on partly in Irish and partly in English. When I visited the school during the past spring a class was in progress in which a lesson in Irish phonetics was being given first in Irish, then in English. The English classes, of course, are carried on through the medium of English, the French through the medium of French, and so forth, but history, geography, science, and similar subjects are taught now in the one language and now in the other. Everybody in the establishment is an Irish-speaker except the cook. The

Clongowes Wood College, Co Kildare, the major Catholic boarding school in Ireland, opened by the Jesuits in 1814.

A front view of the Old Boys Wing (built in 1894) at Coleraine Academical Institution, which opened in 1860. Coleraine was a seventeenth-century, Co Londonderry plantation town, built on an ancient site and developed by the Irish Society, an incorporation of a number of London merchants.

gardener is an especially useful person, as in the hours devoted to nature study he can be turned into a familiar teacher and give easy lessons in the Irish names of the flowers and the trees. Of course, there is a playing-ground where Irish games, like hurling and Gaelic football are played, and there is also a ball-alley – an essentially Irish thing to be found in even the most anti-Irish schools in the country. Tennis is played by the boys during summer.

Robert Lynd

ST ENDA'S COLLEGE

[The following extracts are taken from the Prospectus for St Enda's College, 1913–14.]

Purpose and Scope of College

ST ENDA'S COLLEGE was founded in 1908 with the object of providing for Irish boys a secondary education which, while modern in the best sense, should be distinctively Irish in complexion and bilingual in method. Its programme at once arrested attention, and whether judged by the number of pupils who had come to it, by the satisfaction expressed by their parents with the results of its system, or by the wide and growing reputation it had established, ST ENDA'S had already achieved a remarkable success at the end of its first year. The development of the College during its second year was such as to encourage its founders to remove ST ENDA'S from its original centre at Cullenswood House to a permanent and worthy home – the beautiful and historic demesne known as the Hermitage, a mile beyond the village of Rathfarnham, and a mile and a half from the foot of Kilmashogue mountain, Co. Dublin.

Formation of Character

ST ENDA'S, apart from its distinctively Irish standpoint, has brought the experience of its founders to bear upon an effort to extend the scope and improve the methods of secondary education in Ireland. The central purpose of the College is not so much the mere imparting of knowledge (and not at all the 'cramming' of boys with a view to success at examinations) as the formation of its pupils' characters, the eliciting and development of the individual bents and traits of each, the kindling of their imaginations, and the placing before them of a high standard of conduct and duty. While a wide and generous culture is aimed at, and classical studies are assigned a prominent place in the curriculum, the education provided by the College is on the whole 'modern' in type. . . .

The Course: Irish the Language of the College

In the general curriculum the first place is accorded to the Irish Language, which is taught as a spoken and literary tongue to every pupil. Irish is established as the official language of the College, and is, as far as possible, the ordinary medium of communication between teachers and pupils.

Direct Method Teaching of Modern Languages

All modern language teaching is on the Direct Method. In the class work the teachers keep in view the two-fold object of imparting a *speaking knowledge* and of stimulating an appreciation for literature. French and German are the modern languages taught in addition to Irish and English. Latin is taught to all boys in the upper forms, and Greek to such as exhibit an aptitude for classical studies.

The other subjects are: History, Geography, Nature-Study, Experimental Science (Chemistry and Physics), Mathematics (Arithmetic, Algebra, Euclid, and Trigonometry), Handwriting, Drawing, Manual Instruction, Hygiene and First Aid, Book-keeping, Shorthand, Typewriting, Elocution, Vocal and Instrumental Music, Dancing, and Physical Drill.

Selection of Course

A suitable course is selected for each pupil. In making this selection, not only the wishes of the parents or guardians, but also to a certain extent the wishes and inclinations of the pupil himself are carefully consulted. . . .

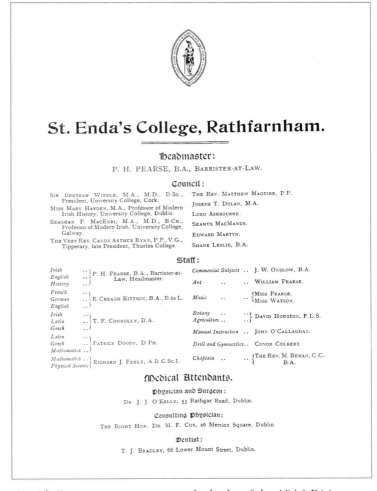

Patrick Pearse, soon to emerge as the leader of the 1916 Rising, was a pioneer of education geared to individual pupils' abilities at his St Enda's College.

Association of Pupils with Administration

The organization of the College embodies some new and important principles. With a view to encouraging a sense of responsiblity among the boys, and establishing between them and the masters a bond of fellowship and *esprit-de-corps*, the pupils are as far as possible actively associated with the administration (though not with the teaching work) of the College. They are consulted with regard to any proposed departures in the curriculum or system of organization, and are frequently called upon for suggestions as to schemes of work or play. At the beginning of each College term they are asked to elect from their own ranks a College Captain, a Vice-Captain, a Secretary, a Librarian, a Keeper of the Museum, a Master of Games, Captains of Hurling nd Football, and a House Committee, their choice being limited merely by the condition that only boys of good conduct are eligible for office. A Branch of the Gaelic League was established in the College during the first term, and its Literary and Debating Society meets regularly.

St Enda's College Prospectus, 1913–14

Trinity College, Dublin: the Campanile. The Rotten Row buildings on the left were demolished to provide student facilities (the Graduate Memorial Building) that were completed in 1902.

TRINITY COLLEGE, DUBLIN

With scenes of well-organized pageantry, the three hundredth anniversary of the Elizabethan foundation was celebrated.

The celebrations began officially with the reception of delegates from home and foreign universities. It was a brilliant scene in the Leinster Hall, Hawkins Street, formerly the site of the old Theatre Royal, and later to be transformed into a theatre once more, when clad in the robes belonging to their respective degrees the delegates filed before the Provost, Dr Salmon, who gave to each a short and happy and often humorous *extempore* greeting. The old Provost was at his very best on the occasion.

Then, after a great procession, there was a fine Commemoration Service in St Patrick's Cathedral, in which the brilliant robes of the visitors, the splendid music, by which the visitors could hardly fail to be impressed, the singing by the general congregation of the metrical version of the ninetieth Psalm, 'O God, our help in ages past' (not to the familiar 'St Anne' tune, but to the traditional local one, 'Irish' or 'Dublin'), all which combined to create a scene which for those who had the privilege of being present was an unforgettable one.

And then there was the evening concert in the Leinster Hall when the Tercentenary Ode, written by Dr Savage Armstrong, and set to music by Sir Robert Stewart, Mus.D., was sung by the augmented choir of the College Choral Society, accompanied by a full orchestra under the baton of the composer. . . .

T.W.E. Drury

QUEEN'S COLLEGE, CORK

Over the arched entrance to the Queen's College are the significant words:

'Where Fin-Barre Taught, Let Munster Learn.'

It is a modern college founded by Queen Victoria in 1849, together with two others of the same sort at Belfast and Galway, and the three are affiliated under the title of 'The Royal University of Ireland'. That gives the degrees bestowed upon their graduates a higher character and a greater value according to the notions of the people here. The buildings are pretentious and of the Tudor order of architecture. They look very much like those of the Washington University at St Louis, and are arranged in a similar manner, only the damp atmosphere here gives the stone a maturity of colour that no college in the United States is old enough to acquire. There are no dormitories. The students room and board where they like. There are only lecture-rooms, examination halls, a library, and a museum. There is no chapel, no religious services, and no bishops or other clergymen are upon the

Queen's College, Galway. The Royal University took over and expanded the function of the Queen's University in 1879. Incorporating the Catholic college in Dublin, it was Ireland's main third-level institution until 1908. Ireland's other university, Trinity College, Dublin, a Protestant foundation of the late sixteenth century, was, like the Royal University, rising to the challenges of both non-denominational and female education as the twentieth century dawned.

board of trustees. That is why the institution is under the ban of the Catholic church . . . There are departments of art, science, engineering, law, and medicine, but no theology. There is a school, at which the applied sciences and the trades are taught, occupying the old building of the Royal Cork Institute and attended by many ambitious young men and women. It is a sort of Cooper Institute, founded by a brewer named Crawford, who made his money here. There is also an agricultural and dairy school, with an experimental farm. . . .

William Eleroy Curtis

QUEEN'S COLLEGE, BELFAST

Indeed, Queen's College, as it was then, was a rather forbidding and comfortless place. The professors for the most part arrived five minutes before lecture-time, talked for an hour, and departed again to the fastnesses of University Street or the Lisburn Road. There were no laboratories or practical work except in chemistry – and for the medical students, of course, anatomy. In each of the three Colleges that constituted the Queen's (later the Royal) University there was a chair of Natural History, the unfortunate occupant of which had to diffuse light on zoology, botany, geology and palaeontology – 'Professors of Creation', as A.C. Haddon used to call them. This is much too

wide a field for any man, and it is not surprising that some of the subjects were treated in a rather perfunctory manner. If you were adrift between lectures, the only place where you could even sit down was on a wooden bench in a small severe room off the main hall, where a silent man with a white beard, as uncommunicative as the Professor of Metaphysics, served plump buns and weak coffee at a reasonable charge. I took geology lectures, necessary for the engineering course, but never handled a rock-specimen or a fossil, though I was allowed to peer at some through the dusty glass of museum cases. But all the time I was fast learning geology and zoology and botany of another kind through the Belfast Naturalists' Field Club.

Robert Lloyd Praeger

DEGREES FOR WOMEN

On January 16, 1904, 'Edward VII, . . . do by these presents authorize and empower the said Provosts and Senior Fellows and their successors in office, and the said Senate of the University of Dublin, and the Caput of the said Senate and all members thereof and all other persons or bodies whose concurrence is necessary for the granting of degrees, to interpret the charter and the statutes of said college in such a manner that women may obtain degrees in the said

Robert Beattie's painting of Queen's University Belfast's Main Building, designed by Charles Lanyon in 1845, shows the building as it might have been in 1912, four years after the original Queen's College had been raised to university status.

University, all previous laws, ordinances, and interpretations notwithstanding.'

Under this authority on May 5, 1904, the board adopted rules admitting women to all lectures, examinations, degrees, and prizes except fellowships and scholarships, their fees being the same as those for men, and all the rules applying to them equally, except that in the medical department 'women shall practice dissection separately from men and medical lectures shall be given them either separately or in conjunction with men, as the professors may think best.'

In June, 1904, the senate also passed 'a grace' for giving degrees to women who had attained a certain prescribed status in the universities of Oxford and Cambridge, and had passed all the examinations and fulfilled all the other requirements for the granting of degrees for men at Trinity.

William Eleroy Curtis

THE DISPENSARY SYSTEM

There are in Ireland 2773 registered medical practitioners. It seems a large number in proportion to the population – a still larger number in proportion to the number of barristers and engineers. In regard to it, it may safely be said that, were it not for the poor-law system, the number of medical practitioners would not be half as great. The salary of a dispensary doctor, small as it seems – in or about £120 a year – in proportion to the work, gives the young doctor something fixed to go on with, and often leads to a remunerative connection. The dispensary system, in this way, places medical assistance within the reach of people, other than the necessitous, who otherwise could not, perhaps, get any medical aid at all.

Michael J.F. McCarthy

COURAGEOUS AND CONSCIENTIOUS

Miss Walshe belongs to the poor, and is kept here by a society with a name of fifteen words – 'Lady Dudley's Scheme for the Establishment of District Nurses in the Poorest Parts of Ireland'. She wears a badge the shape of a heart supporting a crown and in the center is a shamrock leaf encircled with the words of Another One who went about doing good as she does: 'By love serve one another.'

The Countess of Dudley organized this work in 1903, beginning with two nurses in Geesala and Bealadangan, County Galway. And they did so much good that the number has now been increased to fifteen and they are located at as many places in the poorest districts of Ireland, where there are no physicians and where the people are too poor and the population too scattered to support a doctor if one could be induced to go there.

. . . To relieve conditions that may be easily imagined, Lady Dudley's society with the long name was formed, and is now doing an immense amount of good. Fifteen courageous and conscientious women are comfortably placed in localities where their services are most needed, at a cost of not more than a thousand dollars per year each, which includes a bicycle, the most convenient means of locomotion they can find, and an allowance for the hire of horses and jaunting cars when they can be obtained. Because it is impossible to find lodging and boarding places, it has been necessary to build cottages for the nurses, and in some cases the demands upon them are so great that they are allowed to employ assistance. They are equipped with surgical implements and medical stores. Each of the nurses has taken a course in surgery for emergency cases for they are frequently called upon to set bones and dress wounds and even to perform operations. They are also furnished with baby clothes, old linen, warm garments, stores of condensed milk and beef extract, and other delicacies, and although Florence Nightingale relieved thousands, her work did not compare in peril or privation or fatigue with the almost daily experience of some of these noble women.

William Eleroy Curtis

A dispensary, Carnmoney, Co Antrim. This is an example of the basic unit of the largely state-funded Irish health provision, which extended to county fever and mental hospitals from the early decades of the nineteenth century. Subsequently the 1838 Poor Law established 130 union districts each with its own workhouse, some with additional medical facilities.

The Children's Hospital, at the Poor Law Union Workhouse, Lisburn Road, Belfast, during the official opening ceremony, June 1909.

A LOYAL ADDRESS

. . . to commemorate the Diamond Jubilee of Her late Majesty Queen Victoria the citizens resolved to erect a new Hospital, and a sum of over £100,000 was subscribed by them for the purpose. The Construction Committee has now almost finished its labours in the completion and equipment of the Hospital, and will be ready shortly to hand it over to the Board of Management for the use of Patients. Her late Majesty was graciously pleased to allow the New Hospital to be called 'The Royal Victoria Hospital' and to grant a supplemental Charter to the Corporation authorising it in future to take that name. It is this New Hospital which Your Majesties have graciously consented to open to-day, and we tender you on behalf of the Citizens of Belfast, and the Province of Ulster our heartfelt thanks and gratitude for your kindness in coming to perform the ceremony and for the great honour which you have conferred on the Hospital in naming one of the Wards after the late Duke of Clarence, whose memory is held in tender affection by all.

From the 'loyal and dutiful Address of the Construction Committee, the Board of Management and the Medical Staff, Royal Victoria Hospital, Belfast', 27 July 1903

THE WHISKY'S NOT TO BLAME

I visited an insane asylum at Killarney, which is an enormous building, well arranged and equipped with all modern conveniences, under the direction of Dr Edward Griffin, and surrounded by a beautiful garden and hedges in the midst of an estate of sixty acres. It was opened in 1852. The number of inmates in 1908 was 619, of whom 299 were women and 320 men. During the last six or seven years the number of women has largely increased. The average age of the inmates is about thirty years. There are more young men than old men in the institution. Dr Griffin told me that many causes lead to insanity. Whisky, however, has little to do with the condition of the inmates. In 1907 only five men and two women were there for that cause. Tea has a large number of victims, destroying the nervous system by excessive use. The largest proportion come from the counry districts, especially from the seacoast, comparatively few from the towns and cities. The greatest number are of the farming and laboring classes, who made up three-fourths of the inmates received last year – common laborers and poor farmers with two acres of land and two cows. Those from certain districts are generally related, predisposition to insanity being manifest in many families. The farming class, coming from the moors and mountains with their barren soil and great privations, are inclined to insanity because of their impoverished conditions of life. Their only food is often tea, bread, and tobacco. The first treatment at the asylum is to give them plenty of nourishing food and build them up. They are furnished meat every day except Friday. Religious delusions have disturbed the minds of many who fear that they are damned forever and cannot enter heaven. They are hard to cure and the slowest of recovery. The influence of the chaplain in

Asylum attendants of the mental hospital, Co Armagh.

The Dublin Lying-in Hospital (Rotunda), a great maternity hospital with a claim to being the oldest in the United Kingdom, founded by Bartholomew Moss in 1745.

these cases is most beneficial. Under his ministration they receive temporary consolation, but after he has left they often relapse into their former melancholy.

The principal cause of insanity among those who come from the barren moors and desolate mountains is not so much their isolated condition or impoverished life, but their strange delusions. The mountain peasants are very superstitious and imaginative. They believe in fairies and bogies and hear strange voices in the air around them. They believe in leprecawns, which are little men that come out of the ground. They imagine that the fairies and goblins can come through the keyholes of their rooms in the asylum; they are ever hearing strange voices and seeing strange specters as they did upon the moors and mountains.

Of both men and women now in the institution at Killarney more than two hundred have come back to Ireland after a sojourn in America. The superintendent says that the dissipations and excitement of their experience in the United States have caused their mental breakdown after the quiet life and habits of the early days in Ireland. But hereditary predisposition exists in almost every case and in time would have caused the same affliction even though they had remained at home. Hereditary influence and generations of poverty and privation are the general causes of insanity. Very few recoveries are found among those who have been born of insane parents. Most of those dismissed are soon back again, broken down as before by poor nourishment, poverty, and want. The number of readmissions is very large.

William Eleroy Curtis

HOMES FOR THE PEOPLE

The masses of the people live generally in one-storey stone or mud houses, scattered over the long mountain-sides, or clustered in the little one-street villages peculiar to Ireland. Around these houses one generally finds a small garden patch, in which are raised potatoes and other hardy vegetables. In front of the doors are small inclosures, or yards, walled in with stones, sometimes so loosely poised upon each other that one may through the interstices see into the sheep-walks beyond their bounds. Here, around the doorway, the family goat browses; and here the pigs, the geese, and the chickens are wont to gather, indefatigably seeking and as freely obtaining uninterrupted entrance into the living-room of the dwelling.

The interiors of the houses are too often comfortless and bare. It is seldom that more than one room out of a possible two or three has a wooden floor. The others are paved with roughly-fitting flat stones, and are generally cold and damp. In the rural districts there are no stoves or ranges, so cooking is done over the open fire in large fireplaces. Peat is uniformly used for fuel except near the coasts where coal is sometimes imported from Wales. In the interior the use of coal and wood for fuel is unknown.

There are no verandas or porches to the Irish rural or village dwellings; the windows are small square holes made in the thick walls, and stopped with from four to eight panes of glass. Ventilation is unprovided for. Frequently a pigsty or a stable for the cow is inclosed under the same roof of thatch, which is a coating of sedge

Cabin interior. The elderly couple are identified as either Cormac and Kate Holland of Ballyscally townland, Clogher, Co Tyrone, or Patrick and Mary Ann McElroy.

or straw from six inches to a foot in thickness fastened down with ropes.

Such dwellings as described above exist all over Ireland. It is rather remarkable how little variation there is from the type. They are termed 'third class' by the government. The last census shows that there are 251,606 of such in Ireland. The dwellings called 'fourth class' are the lowliest kinds of huts, with dirt floors and one room with one window. There are to-day in remote rural sections of Ireland 9,873 such huts, inhabited by probably thirty or forty thousand people.

The 'second class' houses are of a somewhat better type, especially when found in such cities as Limerick, Cork, Dublin and Belfast. In the better agricultural districts, as in Antrim and Down, Tipperary, Wicklow, and Kilkenny, they may also be found. Many of the second class houses are covered with slate, though in the interior thatch is used. There are 521,000 second class houses in all Ireland. The houses of the 'first class' are the 'castles' of the gentry and landlords scattered through the country and the houses of the

prosperous business and professional men of the cities. There are 75,000 of these in the island.

Plummer F. Jones

HOME IMPROVEMENTS

Mr James Bryce, British Ambassador to Washington, is the author of the act of parliament which authorized a loan of $22,500,000 to build laborers' cottages in Ireland, and under it, according to the latest official returns, 22,500 comfortable new homes have been provided in different parts of the island, and are now occupied by families of farm laborers and other workingmen in the rural districts. Each cottage has from an acre to an acre and one-half of land for a garden. Some of them have barns and other outhouses. They are built of stone and brick of the most substantial character, with roofs of slate or tiles. Most of them have four rooms, two rooms upstairs and two downstairs, with large windows furnishing plenty of light and plenty of ventilation. The cost varies from $750 to $1,000 for a cottage, and is paid by the government with funds derived from the loan mentioned. The tenants pay an average rental of £4 17s. 6d. a year, which is equivalent to about twenty-four dollars in American money or two dollars per month, which covers the interest upon the cost of the cottage, and an installment which will cancel the indebtedness at the end of sixty-eight years. If the tenant owner for whom the cottage is built desires to pay for the property and get a fee simple, he is at liberty to do so at any time, but I did not hear of any such case. Most of the tenants are willing to let their indebtedness run along indefinitely. They can sell, lease, or dispose of the property in any way at any time. The incumbrance goes with the property and not with the man, and is assumed by the purchaser.

It is difficult to overestimate the vast amount of good this movement has accomplished. It is gradually changing the standard of life among the laboring classes throughout Ireland. It has not only furnished comfortable and decent homes for more than twenty-three thousand families, who have been living in miserable, filthy cabins for generations, but it has done much to improve their health. It will strengthen the physical constitutions of the coming generations by placing them in sanitary homes and clean surroundings.

William Eleroy Curtis

LIFE IN POGUE'S ENTRY

The stone cabin was thatch-covered, and measured about twelve by sixteen feet. The space comprised three compartments. One, a bedroom; over the bedroom and beneath the thatch a little loft that served as a bedroom to those of climbing age. The rest of it was workshop, dining-room, sitting-room, parlour, and general community news centre. The old folks slept in a bed, the rest of us slept on the floor and beneath the thatch. Between the bedroom door and the open fireplace was the chimney-corner. Near the door stood an old pine table and some dressers. They stood against the wall and were filled with crockery. We never owned a chair. There were several pine stools, a few creepies (small stools), and a long bench that ran along the bedroom wall, from the chimney-corner to the bedroom door. The mud floor never had the luxury of a covering, nor did a picture ever adorn the bare walls. When the floor needed patching, Jamie went to somebody's garden, brought a shovelful of earth, mixed it and filled the holes. The stools and creepies were scrubbed once a week, the table once a day. I could draw an outline of that old table now and accurately mark every dent and crack in it. I do not know where it came from, but each of us had a *hope* that one day we would possess a pig. We built around the hope a sty and placed it against the end of the cabin. The pig never turned up, but the hope lived there throughout a generation! . . .

When times were good – when work and wages got a little ahead of hunger, which was seldom, Anna baked her own

A very poor cabin in the Mourne Mountains, Co Down.

bread. Three kinds of bread she baked. 'Soda' – common flour bread, never in the shape of a loaf, but bread that lay flat on the gridle; 'pirta oaten' – made of flour and oatmeal; and 'fadge' – potato bread. She always sung while baking, and she sang the most melancholy and plaintive airs. As she baked and sang, I stood beside her on a creepie, watching the process and awaiting the end, for at the close of each batch of bread I always had my 'duragh' – an extra piece. . . .

About ten o'clock the preparations for the big dinner began. We had meat once a week. At least it was the plan to have it so often. Of course, there were times when the plan didn't work, but when it did, Sunday was meat day. The word 'meat' was never used. It was 'kitchen' or 'beef'. Both words meant the same thing, and bacon might be meant by either of them.

In nine cases out of ten, Sunday 'kitchen' was a cow's head, a 'calf's head and pluck', a pair of cow's feet, a few sheep's 'trotters', or a quart of sheep's blood. Sometimes it was the entrails of a pig. Only when there was no money for 'kitchen' did we have blood. It was at first fried and then made part of the broth.

The broth-pot on Sunday was the centre. The economic status of a family could be as easily gauged by tasting their broth as by counting the weekly income. Big money, good broth; little money, thin broth. The slimmer the resource the fewer the ingredients. The pot was an index to every condition and the talisman of every family. It was an opportunity to show off. When Jamie donned a 'dickey' once to attend a funeral and came home with it in his pocket, no comment was made; but if Anna made poor broth it was the talk of the entry for a week.

Good broth consisted of 'kitchen', barley, greens, and lithing. Next to 'kitchen' barley was the most expensive ingredient. Folks in Pogue's Entry didn't always have it, but there were a number of cheap substitutes, such as hard peas or horse beans. Amongst half a dozen families in and around the entry there was a broth exchange. Each family made a few extra quarts and exchanged them. They were distributed in quart tin cans. Each can was emptied, washed, refilled, and returned.

Alexander Irvine

A GOOD INSTITUTION

What can be more agreeable, useful and neighbourly in a country town on its quiet days than a half-door? It shuts out the ground breeze, the stray dog, and many another stray; it shuts in the children, gives a sense of security to the woman of the house while she does a 'hand's turn' in the kitchen; it makes a perch, well out of the reach of dogs, for the

Pogue's Entry, Antrim town, childhood home of Alexander Irvine and which he describes movingly in his tribute to his mother, My Lady of the Chimney Corner, *first published in 1913.*

Ballynahinch Co Down farm interior, showing a woman working at embroidery by the kitchen fireside.

comfortable house cat, and, in idle moments, is the most useful of supports for the good woman's elbows while she has a gossip with the neighbours or takes notes of the passers-by. It is more dignified and respectable than the modern all-open shop doors, for it makes the house appear somehow more its owner's castle, and is, moreover, a prompter to good manners, for, while undoing the latch the visitor has time to think of a 'God save all here', or some such polite self-introduction. Half-doors were a good institution, giving much privacy, yet not setting their faces inhospitably against the world.

Mary Banim

TEA AND CAKE

The house, if it were still in existence, would be a museum piece; a low thatched cottage, a jamb wall between the hall and the kitchen, a living-room at one end of the hall, communicating bedrooms at the other with a bed-in-the-wall in the first, the kitchen with its half-door into 'the street', the scrubbed old dresser, the great open fireplace with its crane, its pots and pans, the turf fire that had glowed and flickered and flamed for centuries, the muzzle loader, with its powder and shot bags and ramrod, over the mantle, and the ladder to the loft where the man or the maid, or both, had their sleeping apartments.

Sides of bacon and ham hung from the ceiling. With what stirring of boyish appetite I would watch my aunt fry the turf-seasoned rashers, and the fresh eggs with sometimes a mushroom or two brought in by my uncle from the early morning dew-soaked fields. With what pleasure I smelt the bubbling yellow meal, and the rich odour of a 'cake' browning in a lidded pan covered with glowing turves. The only beverages were milk, and buttermilk, and tea. Tea! Tea! Tea! There was tea in the morning, tea mid-day, tea after dinner, tea in the afternoon, tea for supper, tea if you came in wet, tea if you came in hungry, tea when visitors arrive, tea at a wake, tea at a wedding. Without tea the world of Gort na Legg, and of Ireland in general, would have collapsed; and the Irish might have been madder than they are. . . .

W. Haughton Crowe

Chapter 7

SOUL: RELIGION IN IRELAND

*R*eligion, long worn as a badge of nationality in Ireland, remained a potent force in the lives of Irish people 100 years ago. Adherence to the Roman Catholic faith had sustained the native Irish and many who had come to reside among them over the centuries and had, in the nineteenth century, increasingly been accepted as one of the characteristics of Irish distinctiveness. This did little to encourage 'Protestant and Dissenter', those with whom the Catholics of the 1798 Rising had wished to unite 'in the common name of Irishmen', to identify with the aspiring Irish nation in 1900. 'Protestants' – the members of the Church of Ireland, disestablished from 1 January 1871 – and 'Dissenters' – Presbyterians largely but including other non-conformists such as Methodists and Quakers (the handier collective 'non-Catholics' was at the time used for all denominations estranged from Rome) – had their own traditions and memories but increasingly found themselves identifying with the Union. That, after all, was a predominantly Protestant kingdom. In Ireland they could only remain a minority among Catholics whom they regarded with suspicion and fear.

Church building, to make up for lost inheritance and the restrictions of an eighteenth-century penal era, characterized Roman Catholic activity in the nineteenth century. Then, after the 1845–9 Famine, Paul Cullen, who dominated the Catholic Church in Ireland during the third quarter of the century, wrought a revolution in discipline and uniform adherence to the practices of Rome, bringing the traditionally relaxed Irish church under central control and overseeing a resurgence in vocations to the priesthood, and to the religious orders, male and female. As the century closed, the hierarchy had committed itself to Home Rule as the only solution to Ireland's political future. The Catholic Church had grown into a self-consciously vibrant force in the land.

While the Church of Ireland was thinly spread throughout the land, Presbyterians were strongest in the North, well organized, with schools and training facilities and with members leading the commercial and industrial life of Ulster. Methodists and Quakers, Baptists and innumerable small sects flourished there also, and the tradition of evangelical proselytizing was strong. Missions and meetings attracted many God-fearing people at a time of intermingled religious and political ferment. The application of the Ne Temere Decree to Ireland by the Roman Catholic Church in 1908, directed as it was to mixed Catholic and non-Catholic marriages and to the upbringing of subsequent children, was to heighten these tensions considerably in the early years of the new century.

Funeral cortège, Co Kerry: mourners carry a coffin through a ruined churchyard, c. 1911.

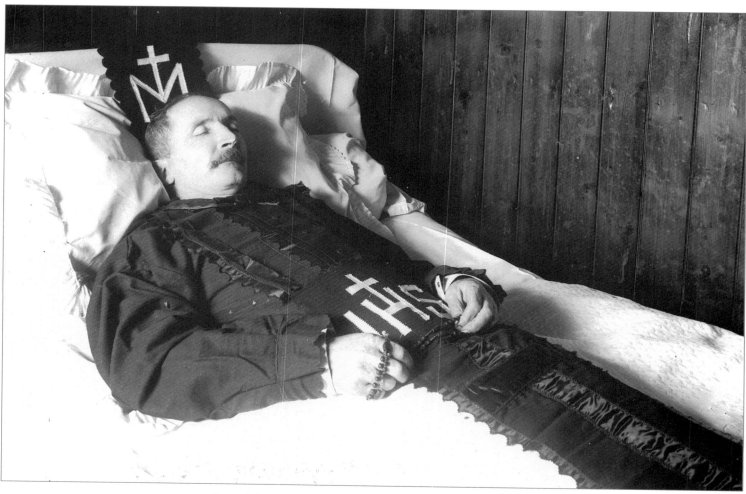

Armagh butcher, Charles Warmall, laid out after death, 1907.

CHURCH STATISTICS

The last official census of the population was taken in 1901. By that census we learn that, barring changes made in the seven years since that time, which do not materially change the proportions, there are 4,458,775 people in the island, of whom 3,308,661 are Catholics, 581,089 Episcopalians, 443,276 Presbyterians, and 61,976 Methodists. There are also a small number of Unitarians, Congregationalists, Baptists, and other scattering sects in the large cities. Of the entire number of Presbyterians, 426,177 live in Ulster, leaving a small remainder of 17,000 scattered through other parts of the island. Of the Episcopalians, 359,898 dwell in Ulster, leaving 222,000 for the rest of the island. It might be stated that this church was formerly the 'Established Church' of Ireland, precisely as the church was also established in England; and it was supported by the Goverment. Mr Gladstone succeeded in having the church disestablished in 1868. The number of Methodists in Ulster is 47,172, leaving about 15,000 for other sections. Offsetting this large number of Protestants in Ulster, there are in that province 699,152 Catholics. . . .

In all Ireland the Catholics constitute 74.20 per cent. of the population; the Episcopalians, 13.03 per cent., the Presbyterians, 9.94 per cent., and the Methodists, 1.39 per cent.

Plummer F. Jones

THIS GOLDEN THREAD . . .

It is a fatal mistake to begin by underestimating the piety of the Irish, or by representing it as an unreal and insincere thing; nothing could be more absurd. It is thoroughly real and sincere. Moreover, at present, it is to thousands of Irish people their only comfort and stay. Through the dark fabric of their lives runs this golden thread of religious faith, standing for them in the place of poetry and art, and of that robuster faith in things as we see them that enlightens more strenuous lives. It is at once their curse and their chief alleviation. It helps them to submit to misery and poverty; and, at the same time, it prevents them from fighting both poverty and misery.

Filson Young

TOWN HALL, PORTADOWN

GENERAL BOOTH
WILL LECTURE
ON MONDAY, MAY 5, 1902,
AT 2.45 P.M.
Subject – 'THE LESSON OF MY LIFE,'

A Salvation army group, possibly pictured at the time of the visit to Portadown of General Booth, 5 May 1902.

Chairman – W.M. Clow, Esq., supported by

Rev. W.J. Macaulay, B.A.
Rev. H.W. Perry, B.A.
Rev. W.Y. Northridge.
Rev. J.W. Parkhill.
Rev. B.S. Lyons.
Messrs.
Geo. M.B. Liddle, M.B.
E.W. Hadden, M.D.
J.C. Fulton, J.P.
Wm Paul, J.P.
D.G. Shillington, J.P.
John Collen, J.P.
C. Courtney, U.D.C.
John Davison, U.D.C.
H. Robb.
J. Young, M.A.
T.H. Spence.
J.B. Bryson.
Jas. M'Kell.
R. Lutton.

A limited number of reserved seats – SIXPENCE.

Sprott Newspaper Collection

A DOUBLE-EDGED SWORD?

Somewhere in Donegal there were two congregations, probably Covenanters, but the exact sect is forgotten. Their meeting-houses were six miles apart. One Congregation held that Christians may fight with the 'Sword of the Lord', the other that Christians may fight with the 'Sword of the Lord, *and of Gideon*'. In both cases the Ministers thought differently from their flocks. So each congregation walked six miles there, and six miles back, to attend the place of worship where their own particular piece of doctrine was preached. They were seen passing each other Sunday after Sunday at the third mile-stone.

Eleanor Alexander

MUSIC AT MULLAVILLY

The annual musical entertainment in connection with Mullavilly Church School was given in the new schoolhouse on Friday evening, when there was a very large attendance. An interesting and varied programme was admirably rendered, the following taking part:– Miss Annie Bell, Miss Jeannie Sprott, Miss Sissie Wilson (Portadown), Miss Lucy Barr, Miss

Mita Dickson, Messrs. O.M. Martin, Graham, Emerson and William Barr, (Tandragee), Master B. Wilson, gold medallist, (Portadown), and the Mullavilly Church Choir. The following acted as accompanists for the evening – Miss Bell, Miss Dickson, and the Rev. Percy Marks, B.A. The proceeds will be devoted to the funds of the Sunday School.

Sprott Newspaper Collection, 16 February 1906

IRISH IRONY

It was in the days of the Band of Hope and the Blue Ribbon movement, and when the fruits of the Father Matthew Teetotal campaign were still ripe, and all Christian denominations in Ireland took some part in combating the intemperance in drink which was then disgracing the land. The Irish Temperance Alliance had arranged a great demonstration in the Antient Concert Rooms in Brunswick street, and the services of a noted temperance (so called) advocate had been secured, Basil Wilberforce, afterwards Archdeacon of Westminster, and Chaplain to the House of Commons. He was the guest at the time of Sir Wm. F. Barrett, F.R.S., a keen temperance reformer.

Opportunity was taken to invite Wilberforce to preach at the afternoon Service at St Patrick's on the Sunday before the great meeting. Visitor and host strolled down to St Patrick's together. 'Who's that?' enquired Wilberforce, as they passed the Benjamin Guinness statue near the south-west door. 'Sir Benjamin Lee Guinness' replied Barrett.

'Anything to do with the brewery?'

'Oh yes,' said Barrett.

'What's he doing there?'

'Why, he was the man who restored this whole Cathedral 30 years ago at a fabulous sum.'

Wilberforce uttered a vehement exclamation, and passed into the Cathedral.

T.W.E. Drury

AN IMPOSING EDIFICE

The new cathedral over which Cardinal Logue presides is also lifted up on high and may be seen from a great distance. The approach is a long flight of steps made of white limestone. The affect is like a Doré illustration of the Apocalypse. One may even fancy the hovering angels in cloud draperies encircling the twin spires. 'Ara Coeli' the situation is appropriately called. I ascended the terraced steps and stood for a while admiring the graceful spires with their surmounting crosses 210 feet above me. Entering the Cathedral I was at once impressed with the richness of the interior and the profuseness of its mosaics. From floor to ceiling were mosaic portrayals of Biblical scenes, with martyrs and Irish saints in mural multitudes. In the pulpit

Caravan of the Faith Mission, an evangelical Protestant mission founded by J.G. Govan (1861–1927) in Edinburgh, in 1886, and extended to the North of Ireland in 1891.

ornamentation St Patrick and St Bridget keep company with the evangelists. The marble altar is of imposing proportions and exquisite workmanship. Behind it is a marvelous marble screen 30 feet wide, 36 feet high upon which is a vivid Crucifixion scene. A beautiful, costly, imposing edifice is the Roman Catholic Cathedral of Armagh. It was commenced in 1840, and was consecrated in 1904 with elaborate ceremonies. In the glitter of its marble, in all the shining glory of its newness it shadows forth the unfading charm of that religion brought to Erin a millennium and a half ago by a Gallic zealot.

Armagh has a parable in its two cathedrals, both commanding supreme positions, the one venerable with an honorable old age, the other mighty in a fresh strength. . . .

W.C. O'Donnell

A BELFAST SABBATH

You hear workingmen discussing theology in the street cars instead of politics, comparing the eloquence of their ministers and their soundness in the faith.

There is a remarkably large attendance at church. All the churches are crowded every Sunday. There is a difference of terms however, with the several denominations. Catholics go to 'mass' where a priest officiates; members of the Church of Ireland attend 'service' which is performed by a parson; while the Presbyterians and other nonconformists go to 'meeting' and hear

the gospel expounded by a minister. The Presbyterian services are very long and heavy. They begin at 11 o'clock on Sunday morning and last till 1:30, and the Sunday school continues two hours. The congregation is never satisfied with a sermon less than an hour long, while an hour and a quarter is preferred, and they insist that their ministers shall expound doctrinal texts to their satisfaction or they criticise them freely and fiercely.

The Irish are the most old-fashioned kind of Presbyterians, being stricter than the Scotch. Few churches allow musical instruments or hymns that rhyme, and the congregations follow a precentor with a tuning fork in chanting Rouse's version of the Psalms of David.

The people remember the Sabbath day to keep it holy only until afternoon. There are no railway trains or street cars running in the morning, and you cannot find a cab or a jaunting car on the street. . . .

William Eleroy Curits

EPISCOPAL APPROBATION

In the Pastoral Letter of His Eminence Cardinal Logue for Lent, 1902, we find the following:– 'A great work is being done by the Catholic Truth Society of Ireland for furnishing the people with such reading as will deprive them of all excuse for resorting to the poisoned sources from which so many were wont to imbibe an irreligious, sensual, and often corrupting

Regarded as Ireland's most important Patrician site, Armagh is the seat of the Roman Catholic and Protestant (Church of Ireland) Archibishops. Its two cathedrals are here shown, the smaller Protestant cathedral dating from the thriteenth century, the larger Catholic cathedral having been built between 1840 and 1873.

Michael Logue (1840–1924), Roman Catholic Archbishop of Armagh in 1888, Cardinal in 1893. He is pictured here in 1900.

William Alexander (1824–1911), Church of Ireland Archbishop of Armagh and Primate of all Ireland from 1896 to 1911. Husband of the distinguished hymn writer C.F. Alexander, and a noted preacher, he is pictured here c. 1890.

draught. *Their efforts merit and should receive every support.* Whenever I see in a church the well-known box destined for the distribution of their publications, I take it as a clear proof of the pastor's zeal for the best interests of his people.'

In the Lenten Regulations for the Diocese of Dublin 1903, His Grace the Archbishop writes:– 'The work of the Catholic Truth Society [Ireland], now so firmly established and happily so successful throughout the diocese, *is deserving of every encouragement from both clergy and laity.*'

'It is well known,' writes His Grace the Archbishop of Tuam, 'that various printing presses in Great Britain daily pour out a flood of infidel and immoral publications some of which overflows to this country. We have a confident hope that the Society's [C.T.S.I.] publications will remove the temptation of having recourse to such filthy garbage, will create a taste for pure and wholesome literature, and will also serve as an antidote against the poison of dangerous or immoral writings.'

'Allow me, dearly beloved,' writes Dr Fennelly, Archbishop of Cashel, in his Lenten Pastoral, 1903, 'before concluding, to say something in favour of the Catholic Truth Society, which has been got up for the purpose of counteracting a growing taste amongst our people for an overflow of filthy literature from England and other countries. Its publications are racy of the soil; are very varied in point of subject; and, as far as I can

judge, are, in many instances, of high literary merit. *I ask priests and people to support the Catholic Truth Society by taking and reading its publications.'*

Catholic Truth Society of Ireland, 1903

St Patrick's Pilgrims

We are looking eastward, from Station Island, over the waters of Lough Derg toward the bleak Donegal hills. Immediately before us, a group of pilgrims kneel, bare-headed, and with shoes removed, before a little iron cross, on a twisted pillar of stone. In coming here, they are making a pilgrimage to one of the oldest shrines in western Europe, one to which pilgrims flocked for centuries before the murder of Thomas à Becket called forth the Canterbury Pilgrims; one which remains a place of pilgrimage to-day, after Canterbury has ceased for centuries to draw pious pilgrims. Here is the tradition of this island shrine:

During one of his journeys to the west, Saint Patrick withdrew to this lonely isle in a lonely lake, amid lonely mountains. He was one day deep in prayer, when lo! before his heaven-touched fancy the regions of purgatory sprang into existence, and he saw the souls of millions undergoing the

Pilgrims embark for Lough Derg, Co Donegal, place of devotion, penance, fasting and dedication to St Patrick, Ireland's Patron Saint. Dating from the thirteenth century, it is still an active site of pilgrimage, especially in the months of July and August.

The Sanctuary, Lough Derg (St Patrick's Purgatory). The popularity of this place of pilgrimage grew as part of the devotional revolution that marked the Irish Catholic Church, especially from the mid-nineteenth century onwards.

process of purification. Saint Patrick, awed by the vision, departed from the cave, and ordered that henceforth the island should be a terrestrial Purgatory, where sinners could 'wash off all their sins by prayer and fasting'. A disciple of Saint Patrick, Daveog by name, founded a monastery here, in the fifth century, and even at that early date the stream of pilgrims had begun to flow. This first monastery was destroyed by the Danes in the ninth century, the epoch of the Round Towers. In the twelfth century, a learned English Benedictine monk wrote a description of the pilgrimage hither of a certain Louis Owain, and the great Spanish dramatist Calderon later turned it into a play. The Norman kings paid veneration to this shrine, and great personages came from the Continent, to visit it. A hostile report led to its condemnation by one of the Popes, but it was soon restored to favor. In the seventeenth and eighteenth centuries, it was attacked by the English authorities, but its sacred renown is still as strong as ever.

The pilgrims come here from the beginning of June till the middle of August, the services culminating on August 15, the Feast of the Assumption, which the country people call 'Lady Day in harvest', to distinguish it from 'Lady Day in Spring', the Feast of the Annunciation. The pilgrims stay three, six or nine days, according to the period of purification they have chosen, finding shelter for the night at the Hospice, which, with the Chapels of Saint Patrick and Saint Mary, and the Presbytery, make up the group of buildings on this island. Their days are passed in prayer in the chapels, or before this

Cross of Saint Patrick; and each day they have one meal of dry bread and weak tea. In olden days there was a cave on the island, within which Saint Patrick was praying when he had his vision, but it is now closed up.

Charles Johnston

COPIOUS CONVENTS

The great wall of the convent confronted me. I wonder where all the money comes from?

Out of Purgatory's bank, Conan answered cheerfully; and there is no fear of them overdrawing their account, for money is always dribbling in. Nothing thrives in Ireland like a convent, a public-house, and a race-meeting. Any small house will do for a beginning; a poor-box is put in the wall, a couple of blind girls are taken in, and so salubrious is our climate that the nuns find themselves in five years in a Georgian house situated in the middle of a beautiful park. The convent whose music distracts your meditations is occupied by Loreto nuns – a teaching order, where the daughters of Dublin shopkeepers are sure of acquiring a nice accent in French and English. St Vincent's Hospital, at the corner, is run by nuns who employ trained nurses to tend the sick. The eyes of the modern nun may not look under the bedclothes; the medieval nun had no such scruples. Our neighbourhood is a little overdone in

Croaghpatrick (2,500 ft) from Westport, Co Mayo, one of Ireland's main places of pilgrimage, especially on the last Sunday of July. Note also the goods wagons of the Midland Great Western Railway in the foreground, the line from Castlebar (of the then Great Northern and Western Railway, which amalgamated with the MGWR in 1890) opening in 1866.

convents; the north side is still richer. But let's count what we have around us: two in Leeson Street, one in Baggot Street and a training college, one in Ballsbridge, two in Donnybrook, one in Ranelagh; there is a convent at Sandymount, and then there is John Eglinton's convent at Merrion; there is another in Booterstown. Stillorgan Road is still free from them; but I hear that a foreign order is watching the beautiful residences on the right and left, and as soon as one comes into the market . . .

George Moore

AT A TRAPPIST RETREAT

After vespers came 'tea', which I had supposed would be literally nothing else, but there was the most delicious graham bread I have had since I came to Ireland, and unlimited milk. There was no butter, as it was a fast day. This I regretted keenly.

Talk went on among us all until a bearded monk in white came in and began to read passages from Thomas à Kempis. His enunciation was peculiarly pure, and I doubt not that he was a gentleman born. It was a pleasure to hear such English. While he read we were all silent.

After supper we went out to the garden, and in a sheltered place (although we did not need a shelter, as the fickle rain had stopped) those who wished played a spirited game that consisted of tossing stones into a little pocket of earth. One of the priests was an adept, and he carried all before him.

In such simple pleasures, or in walking, the evening was spent until it came time to go to chapel again. . . .

At eight I sought my room, where there was reading matter suitable to the place, but the candle was not conducive to extended reading unless I held it close to the book, and then it dazzled me, and at nine o'clock I was in my bed, and until two in the morning the house was quiet, save for a snore here and there. But at two the bells began to ring, and kept it up at intervals all through the night. . . .

I was up at six, but it was some time after that that I heard steps in the hall. I had looked out of the window from time to time, hoping to see some one in the garden. The table of the duties of the day hung in my room, and I noticed that breafast was at nine. . . .

But before eight the good father came and asked me if I'd like to see the interior of the monastery, and he showed me the bakeshop with its most up to date ovens, and oh, how hungry the smell of baking made me, and the steam-saw, and the creamery, and the library. . . .

Doon holy well, Kilmacrenan, Co Donegal, showing rags tied to surrounding bushes. This was the traditional way to mark prayers for recovery from illness, deformity or disability.

Corpus Christi Day, Youghal, Co Cork in the early 1900s: the procession receives Benediction at the park bandstand, before returning to church.

At breakfast there were eggs and milk and tea, and delicious butter in abundance, and the reading of some holy book by Father David, which did not stop all conversation. Being a feast day, there was one priest who felt his tongue could be loosened, and he kept up an under-current of conversation, to Father David's annoyance, but it was a human touch that was not out of place.

The monks are themselves vegetarians, but a school is run in connection with the monastery, and the students are allowed meats.

C.B. Loomis

THE MATCH-MAKING BUSINESS

It is unlucky to marry for love, according to an Irish proverb. Ireland, if one can trust the general belief, is a land of marriages of convenience rather than of marriages of romance, and undoubtedly it is also a land of happy marriages. . . .

Match-making, of course, is known in every country where money is reverenced, and it is not only in Ireland that men marry with an eye to a dowry. Still, Irish match-making is a distinct institution. It is not an unheard-of, though it is an uncommon thing in rural Ireland for the woman never to have seen the man she is going to marry until he calls at her father's house to take away the dowry. Cases even have been known where the girl had not set eyes on her husband till the marriage-morning. The marriage is frequently arranged without any

reference to her tastes and wishes. Her father comes home one evening and tells her that he has got a husband for her, and she can but wait in patience and wonder till the young man calls.

Marriages like these are brought about by a curious machinery. It is often difficult to know who first suggests them. Sometimes, it is an old busy-body with an appetite for glory. He casts his glance at a young girl and learns by some means or other the amount of the fortune which her father is willing to give with her. After this, he puzzles his brains to find a suitable husband. He picks out some farmer of substance and broaches the matter to him in hints, say, during a drink at a fair. If the farmer seems inclined for the marriage, the match-maker goes off and arranges a conference between him and the girl's father. It is then the bargaining begins, the girl's father doing his utmost to lessen his prospective son-in-law's demands by it may be fifty sovereigns or it may be a cow. Indecent scenes of heat and miserly excitement in connection with these preliminary meetings are a favourite subject with Irish novelists, and indeed there is plenty of material both for satire and tragedy in the match-making business. Still, I think the novelists exaggerate the dark side. If the custom were altogether cruel and selfish in practice, Irish homes would not be so full of a pleasant atmosphere of affectionateness as they usually are.

As a matter of fact, the custom of match-making does not often seem to involve the forcing of husbands on unwilling girls, as we might at first think would be probable. Girls, I imagine are not forced into marriage against their will in Ireland more frequently than in other countries. If the girl is not always at liberty to choose a husband, she is generally at liberty to refuse a husband she does not want.

Robert Lynd

THE WILD KEEN

While the grave was being opened the women sat down among the flat tombstones, bordered with a pale fringe of early bracken, and began the wild keen, or crying for the dead. Each old woman, as she took her turn in the leading recitative, seemed possessed for the moment with a profound ecstasy of grief, swaying to and fro, and bending her forehead to the stone before her, while she called out to the dead with a perpetually recurring chant of sobs.

All round the graveyard other wrinkled women, looking out from under the deep red petticoats that cloaked them, rocked themselves with the same rhythm, and intoned the inarticulate chant that is sustained by all as an accompaniment.

The morning had been beautifully fine but as they lowered the coffin into the grave, thunder rumbled overhead and hailstones hissed among the bracken.

In Inishmaan one is forced to believe in a sympathy between man and nature, and at this moment when the thunder sounded a death-peal of extraordinary grandeur above the voices of the women, I could see the faces near me stiff and drawn with emotion.

When the coffin was in the grave, and the thunder had rolled away across the hills of Clare, the keen broke out again more passionately than before.

This grief of the keen is no personal complaint for the death of one woman over eighty years, but seems to contain the whole passionate rage that lurks somewhere in every native of the island. In this cry of pain the inner consciousness of the people seems to lay itself bare for an instant, and to reveal the mood of beings who feel their isolation in the face of a universe that wars on them with winds and seas. They are usually silent, but in the presence of death all outward show of indifference or patience is forgotten, and they shriek with pitiable despair before the horror of the fate to which they all are doomed.

Before they covered the coffin an old man kneeled down by the grave and repeated a simple prayer for the dead.

There was an irony in these words of atonement and Catholic belief spoken by voices that were still hoarse with the cries of pagan desperation.

John M. Synge

AN ANTRIM WAKE

He died suddenly, and Eliza, his mother, came at once for help to the chimney-corner.

'He's gone, Anna, he's gone!' she said, as she dropped on the floor beside Anna.

'An' ye want me t' do fer yer dead what ye'd do for mine, 'Liza?'

'Ay, ay, Anna, yer God's angel to yer frien's.'

'Go an fetch 'Liza Conlon, Jane Burrows, and Marget Houston!' was Anna's order to Jamie.

The women came at once. The plan was outlined, the labour apportioned, and they went to work. Jamie went for the carpenter and hired William Gainer to dig the grave. Eliza Conlon made the shroud, Jane Burrows and Anna washed and laid out the corpse, and Mrs Houston kept Eliza in Anna's bed until the preliminaries for the wake were completed. . . .

Eliza Conlon abruptly terminated the conversation by announcing that all was ready for the wake.

'Ah, but it's the purty corpse he is,' she said, '– luks jist like life!'

The three women went over to the Lecky home. It was a one-room place. The big bed stood in the corner. The corpse was 'laid-out' with the hands clasped.

The moment Eliza entered she rushed to the bed and fell on her knees beside it. She was quiet, however, and after a moment's pause she raised her head and laying a hand on the folded hands, said: 'Ah, han's ov God t' be so cold an' still!'

Anna stood beside her until she thought she had stayed long enough, then led her gently away. From that moment Anna directed the wake and the funeral from her chimney-corner.

'Here's a basket ov flowers for Henry, Anna, the childther gethered thim th' day,' Maggie McKinstry said, as she laid them down on the hearthstones beside Anna.

'Ye've got some time, Maggie?'

'Oh, ay.'

'Make a chain ov them an' let it go all th' way aroun' th' body, they'll look purty that way, don't ye think so?'

A death card, much in vogue in this era, here referring to Mary Archbold, Co Antrim, June 1905.

'Illigant, indeed, to be shure! 'Deed I'll do it.' And it was done.

To Eliza Conlon was given the task of providing refreshments. I say 'task', for after the carpenter was paid for the coffin and Jamie Scott for the hearse there was only six shillings left.

'Get whey for th' childther,' Anna said, and 'childther' in this catalogue ran up into the twenties.

For the older 'childther' there was something from Mrs Lorimer's public-house – something that was kept under cover and passed around late, and later still diluted and passed around again. Concerning this item Anna said: 'Wather it well, dear, an' save in their wits; they've got little enough now, God save us all!' . . .

Shortly after midnight Anna went over to see how things were at the wake. They told her of the singing of the children, of the beautiful chapther by Misther Gwynn, and the 'feelin' prayer by Graham Shannon. The whey was sufficient and nearly everybody had 'a dhrap o' th' craither' and a bite of fadge.

'Ah Anna dear,' Eliza said, 'shure it's yerself that knows how t' make a moi'ty go th' longest distance over dhry throats an' empty stomachs! 'Deed it was a revival an' a faste in wan, an' th' only pity is that poor Henry cudn't enjoy it!'

YMCA, Wellington Hall, Wellington Place, Belfast: a convention in the Minor Hall with Sir James Musgrave (1826–1904), leading businessman, philanthropist and Donegal landowner, on the platform.

The candles were burned low in the sconces, the flowers around the corpse had faded, a few tongues, loosened by stimulation, were still wagging, but the laughter had died down and the stories were all told. There had been a hair-raising ghost story that had sent a dozen home before the *respectable* time of departure. The empty stools had been carried outside and were largely occupied by lovers.

Anna drew Eliza's head to her breast, and pressing it gently to her, said, 'I'm proud of ye, dear, ye've borne up bravely! Now I'm going' to have a few winks in th' corner, for ther'll be much to do the morra.'

Alexander Irvine

PAYING ONE'S RESPECTS

A poor old widow, a neighbour of ours, in a lonely cabin, had died suddenly, and was to be buried in a burying ground some ten miles away over the hills. We would have wished to have paid our respects by following the *cortége*; but, alas! Betsy had done her best for us, and could do no more. Possibly it turned out for the best, for we learnt that those who followed the remains were expected to dig the grave, as there was no resident sexton in this mountain cemetery, and of this operation we were as inexperienced as a

baby in arms. Even F.R.B., who is a handy man at most things, would have been a long way off figuring as a respectable sexton.

Revd Charles Kent

SPIRIT-FILLED OCCASIONS?

The Roman Catholic clergy are doing a great deal to suppress disorder and promote temperance by prohibiting the use of liquor at wakes. Cardinal Logue and the several archbishops and bishops are determined to abolish the disgraceful orgies that have been so common on such occasions, and have forbidden priests to officiate at funerals or even to say masses for the souls of the dead where liquor is offered to the neighbors and mourners who sit up with the corpse. Some of the bishops require the remains to be brought to the church on the day before the funeral. As a consequence, the scandalous custom of holding a carousal the night before the funeral is almost entirely obsolete except in the slums of the large cities and in remote rural districts. As a rule throughout Ireland, where friends now gather to 'sit up' with the corpse as a token of respect and sorrow, they are furnished with no stronger refreshments than tea.

William Eleroy Curtis

Photographic Credits & Text Sources

Acknowledgements

I am indebted to many librarians, scholars and individual photo enthusiasts but my principal thanks are due to The Bradley Institute for Democracy and Public Values, Marquette University, Milwaukee, for the Fellowship that gave me the time for much of the preparation of this book, to Tom Hachey, Director, and to Dawn Crowley, Administrator. I also wish to thank the librarians of the Memorial Library of that fine university, and Sean Keane, Mary ni Chuillinain and Cathy Flanagan, and The American Irish Historical Society, New York. My thanks go also to The Institute of Irish Studies, Queen's University (Brian Walker, Sophia King, Margaret McNulty, Bill Crawford and especially Catherine Boone); to the University's photographers (Ivan Ewart and Martin Boyd); to the University Library (Michael Smallman), and to numerous individuals in The National Museums and Galleries of Northern Ireland (Pauline Dickson, Trevor Parkhill, Vivienne Pollock, Sally Skillen, Jonathan Bell, and Ken Anderson); The National Library of Ireland (Sylvia Lynham, Grainne McLaughlin and, not least, Pat Donlon, former Director); The Linenhall Library, Belfast (John Killen); The Public Record Office, NI (David Lammey and Ian Montgomery); The Boole Library, University College Cork (Carol Quinn and Aoife ni Bhraoin); The Cork Public Museum (Stella Cherry), and The Cork Butter Museum (Colin Rynne); The Cobh Museum (Heather and David Bird); *Cork Examiner* (Lilian Caverley); Cork Public Library (Tim Cadogan); the Governors of Victoria College, Belfast (and Mrs Hughes); and of Portadown College (and Robert Lobb, custodian of the Sprott Collection); the Horgan family (Jim in Galway, Joan and Tom Collins, Ballymacask, Youghal); and Joe Wilson (Cobh); Willie Wallace (NIFCC), and Joan McCloy (ILHU), and husband John; to Professor Trevor West (TCD); David Berkeley (ICOS); J.J. Kett (UCC); and Margaret Ballantine (DoE NI).

Illustrations

The photographs and paintings are hereby credited with grateful thanks to: The Trustees of The National Museums and Galleries of Northern Ireland: a) Ulster Museum: Welch Collection: ii, v, 2, 6, 9, 13, 23, 28, 31, 42, 46, 50 (top, middle), 55 (bottom), 56, 57, 58 (bottom), 60 (top), 63 (bottom), 64, 68, 69 (top), 70 (top), 74, 80, 84, 88, 96, 100, 104, 106, 115, Hogg Collection: 7 (top), 25, 58 (top), 82, 94, 118, Bigger Collection: 4, 52, 63 (top), 70 (bottom), Langham Collection: courtesy Lady Langham: vi (top); b) Ulster Folk and Transport Museum: W.A. Green Collection: i, 3, 7 (bottom), 8, 11, 12, 16, 19, 20, 24, 30, 32, 40, 43, 44, 45, 50 (bottom), 51, 59, 60 (bottom), 61, 62, 65, 66 (top), 81, 105, Harland & Wolff Collection: vi (middle), 53, 54, Ferguson Collection: 10, 15, Dundee Collection: front cover, 99, 117, Rose Shaw Collection: 103, Education Department: 90; The National Library of Ireland: Lawrence Collection: courtesy The National Library of Ireland: 5, 26, 27, 29, 79, 92, 93, 97, 102, 113, 114; The Public Record Office of Northern Ireland, with permission of The Deputy Keeper of the Records: Cooper Collection: iv, 17, 18, 35, 39, 55 (top), 71, 75, 83 (top), 85, 110, Allison Collection: 47, 48, 83 (bottom), 89, 101, 108, 111, 112; The Sprott Collection, Portadown College: 1, 32 (top right), 37, 72, 73 (top), 109; Linen Hall Library, Belfast: 32 (top left), 36, 41, 86; Horgan Collection (Youghal): back cover (top), iii, 87 (bottom), 116; Cork City Museum (photographer Tony Balfe): 34; *Cork Examiner*: vi (bottom); University College, Cork: back cover (bottom), 76 (top), 87 (top), 107; Cobh Museum: 76 (bottom); *Punch*: 4, 21, 22, 33 (bottom); Irish Co-operative Organisation Society: 32 (bottom left & right), 33 (top); Borde Failte: 69 (bottom); Wilson Collection (Cobh): 73 (bottom); North of Ireland Football and Cricket Club: 77, 78; Victoria College, Belfast: 91; R.D. Beattie (by whose kind permission his painting is reproduced): 98; *Illustrated London News*: 66 (bottom).

Texts

I have made every effort to contact all copyright holders, but in some cases this has proved impossible and I apologise to any who have been overlooked. The sources that follow are credited, with thanks to the copyright owners, their heirs and successors. They are listed in order of first appearance in the text. William Charles O'Donnell, *Around the Emerald Isle: A Record of Impressions* (Roxborough, 1910); Madame de Bovet, *Three Months in Ireland*, translated by Mrs Arthur Walter (Harper, 1902); Plummer F. Jones, *Shamrock Land: A Ramble through Ireland* (Moffat, Yard, 1909); Michael Myers Shoemaker, *Wanderings in Ireland* (Putnam, 1908); Alfred Austin, *Spring and Autumn in Ireland* (Blackwood, 1900); John M. Synge, *The Aran Islands* (OUP, 1907); Alexander Corkey, *The Truth about Ireland: or Through the Emerald Isle with an Aeroplane* (Shockley Bros and Cooke, 1910); R.A. Scott-James, *An Englishman in Ireland: Impressions on a Journey in a Canoe, by River, Lough and Canal* (Dent, 1910); William Eleroy Curtis, *One Irish Summer* (Duffield, 1909); Walter Long, *Memories* (Hutchinson, 1923); Florence Mary McDowell, *Roses and Rainbows* (Appletree, 1972); W. Houghton Crowe, *Beyond the Hills: an Ulster Headmaster Remembers* (Dundalgan Press, 1971); Percy French, *Are Ye Right There Michael*; Hector Bolitho, *Victoria, the Widow and her Son* (Cobden-Sanderson, 1934); W.B. Yeats, letters, to *The Freemans Journal*, 20 March and 4 April 1900 (by kind permission of Mr Michael Yeats); Michael J.F. McCarthy *Five Years in Ireland: 1895–1900* (Hodges Figgis, 1903); James Pope-Hennessy, *Lord Crewe: the Likeness of a Liberal* (Constable, 1955); J.W. Mackail and Guy Wyndham, *Life and Letters of George Wyndham* (Hutchinson, 1925); General Sir Alexander Godley, *Life of an Irish Soldier* (John Murray, 1939); David Fitzpatrick in Tom Bartlett and Keith Jeffery (eds), *A Military History of Ireland* (CUP, 1996); John D. Brewer, *The RIC: an Oral History* (Institute of Irish Studies, 1990: by kind permission of the author); Harold Nicolson (and quotation from Alfred Lord Tennyson), *Helen's Tower* (Constable, 1937: by kind permission of Nigel Nicolson); Sir Horace Plunkett, letter to *Irish Homestead* (1895) and *Ireland in the New Century* (1902/3); Robert McElborough, unpublished 'Autobiography of a Belfast Workingman' by kind permission of The Deputy Keeper of Records, Public Record Office of Northern Ireland; Robert Lynd, *Home Life in Ireland* (Mills and Boone, 1910: all references, save p. 46, which is from *Irish and English, Portraits and Impressions*, Francis Griffith, 1908); Alan Denison (ed.), *Letters from AE* (Abelard Schuman, 1961); Lynn Doyle, *Ballygullion* (Blackstaff reprint of 1908 edn); Charles Johnston, *Ireland through the Stereoscope* (Underwood and Underwood, 1907); Robert Moreton, *Come Day, Go Day, God Send Sunday* (Routledge and Kegan Paul, 1973); George Russell (AE), *Irish Review* (1911–12); F.G. Hall, *The Bank of Ireland, 1783–1946* (Hodges Figgis, 1949: by kind permission of the Governors); Mary Banim, *Here and There through Ireland* (*Freeman's Journal*, 1891); Robert Lloyd Praeger, *The Way that I Went* (Hodges Figgis, 1937: by kind permission of Mr Neville Figgis); Stephen Gwynne, *The Fair Hills of Ireland* (Maunsel, 1906); George Moore, *Hail and Farewell* (1914: Colin Smythe edn, 1976); Daniel Lewis, *The Province of Ulster* (H.J. Ronalds, 1896); William Alexander Houston Collisson, *In and On Ireland* (Sutton, 1908); Douglas Hyde, address to the Gaelic League, 1892 (by kind permission of Mr Douglas Sealy); H.B., *Letters from Ireland* (*New Ireland Review*, 1902); Michael McGowan, *The Hard Road to Klondyke*, translated by Valentin Iremonger (Routledge and Kegan Paul, 1962); Hubert Butler, *In the Land of Nod* (Lilliput, 1996); Denis Ireland, *From the Jungle of Belfast* (Blackstaff, 1972); Brian Walker and Alf McCreary, *Degrees of Excellence* (Institute of Irish Studies, 1994); Edward MacLysaght, *Changing Times: Ireland since 1898* (Colin Smythe, 1978); Herbert Maxwell in Cosmopolite, *The Sportsman in Ireland* (Edward Arnold, 1897 edn); Revd Charles Kent, *By Celtic Waters* (J. Davy, 1894); Gifford Lewis (ed.), *The Selected Letters of Somerville and Ross* (Faber, 1989);

Revd Dr O. Loughlin and J.R. Campbell in *The Victoria College Magazine*, No. 46, 1902; Albert LeRoy Bartlett, *A Golden Way; Being Notes and Impressions of a Journey through Ireland, Scotland and England* (Abbey Press, 1901); Mrs Faris, *The Victorian*, No. 44 (1959); T.W.E. Drury, *Unforgotten* (APCK, 1951); *Prospectus, St Enda's College* (1913–14); Robert Marshall,

Fifty Years on the Grosvenor Road (RVH, 1951); Alexander Irvine, *My Lady of the Chimney Corner* (Blackstaff reprint of original 1913 edn); Filson Young, *Ireland at the Cross Roads* (Grant Richards, 1904); Eleanor Alexander, *Primate Alexander: Archbishop of Armagh* (Edward Arnold, 1913); Charles Battel Loomis, *Just Irish* (Gorham Press, 1909).

INDEX

Achill Island, Co Mayo, 7
Aghascrebagh, Co Tyrone, i
Aird, near Giant's Causeway, 88
Alexander, William, Archbishop, 112
Alexandra College, Dublin, 88, 92, 93
Aran, 9, 41
Ardara, Co Donegal, 50
Ardglass, Co Down, 51
Armagh, 111
Auburn, Co Westmeath, 4

Ballindrait, Co Donegal, 17
Ballycastle, Co Antrim, 74
Ballynahinch, Co Down, 55, 106
Ballynahinch, Co Galway, 3
Bangor, Co Down, 80
Bann, River, 16
Belfast, viii, 4, 11, 25, 36, 53, 82, 100, 118
Belleek Pottery, Co Fermanagh, ii, 4
Boyne, River, 65

Carlingford, 2
Carnmoney, Co Antrim, 99
Cashel, Co Tipperary, 64
Clandeboye House, Co Down, 29, 30
    Helen's Tower, 30
Clongowes Wood College, Co Kildare, 93
Clonmacnoise, Co Offaly, 56
Cloughroe National School, north-west Ulster, 89
Coleraine Academical Institution, 94
Conagher, Dervock, Co Antrim, 9
Connemara, 4, 11
Connolly, James, 20
Cookstown, Co Tyrone, 43
Cork, 4, 13
Cove (Queenstown), later Cobh, 76
Crebilly House, near Ballymena, 58
Croaghpatrick, 114
Croke, Archbishop, 71
Cuchulainn, statue of, 69
Cullen, Paul, 107
Curragh, The, 24, 26
Currie, Sir Donald, vi
Cusack, Michael, 71

Derg, Lough, Co Donegal, 113
Doon holy well, Kilmacrenan, Co Donegal, 115
Dublin, ii, vii, viii, 4, 8, 23, 24, 73, 102
Dudley, Countess of, 99
Dufferin, Frederick, Marquis of, 30
Dugort, Achill Island, Co Mayo, 7
Dun Leary (Dun Laoghaire), 5
Dundalk, Co Louth, 47
Dunlop, John, 74
Dunluce Castle, 19

Edward VII, 25

Ferguson, Harry, 10, 15
fishing, 3, 81

Gaelic Athletic Association, 56, 71
Gaelic League, 56, 82, 95
Galway, 26
Giant's Causeway, Co Antrim, 19
Goldsmith, Oliver, 4
golf, 3, 71, 74
Green, W.A., 40
Gregory, Lady, 56, 67, 68
Griffith, Arthur, 20, 32
Groomsport, Co Down, v

Harland and Wolff shipyard, vi, 53, 54
Henry, Mitchel, 20
Herdman Brothers, 55, 75
horse-racing, 24
Hyde, Douglas, 56

Inishmore, Aran Islands, 58, 68, 69
Irish Agricultural Organization Society, 38
Irish Field Clubs Union, 56
Irish Literary Theatre, 71
Irvine, Alexander, 105

'jaunting' car, 3, 7, 14
Jerpoint Abbey, Knocktopher, 63

Killarney, 2, 10
Kilmacrenan, Co Donegal, 115
Knocktopher, Co Kilkenny, 63

Kylemore Castle, Co Galway, 11, 20

Lagan, River, 12
Lambin's tobacco factory, Cork, vi
language and literature, vii, 56, 64, 66, 94
Larkin, James ('Big Jim'), 20, 36
Lee, Sam, 77
Lifford, Co Donegal, 18
Limerick, 4, 27
linen, 38, 44, 45, 53, 55, 81
Logue, Michael, Cardinal, 112, 118
Lough Gur, Co Limerick, 61

McKinley, William, 9
MacNeill, Eoin, 56, 67
McSwiggin, Mathew (public house), Ulster, iv
Martin, Violet, 3
Martyn, Edward, 56, 67
Moore, George, 67
Mourne Mountains, Co Down, 2, 81, 104
Moy National School, 90
Muredath's Cross, Monasterboice, Co Louth, 62
Murlough Bay, Co Antrim, 57
Musgrave, Sir James, 118

Nangle, Revd Edward, 7
Neagh, Lough, Co Antrim, 44, 84
New Grange, Co Meath, 59
Newry, Co Down, 48

O'Connell, Daniel (the Liberator), 8
O'Grady, Standish, 56, 67
O'Growney, Father Eugene, 56
O'Neill Arms Hotel, Toome, Co Antrim, 6
Ogham Stone, i
Oldbridge, Co Meath, 65
Oughter, Lough, Co Cavan, 80

Pirrie, W.J., vi
Plunkett, Horace, vii, 33, 38, 39
Pogue's Entry, Antrim town, 105
Portadown, Co Antrim, 73
    Portadown Foundry workers, 1

Portrush, Co Antrim, 6, 7, 84
Praeger, Robert Lloyd, 42

Queen's College, Cork, 13, 96
Queen's College, Galway, 96, 97
Queen's University, Belfast, viii, 97, 98
Queenstown (Cove), 10

Raphoe, Co Donegal, 35
Redmond, John, 20, 22, 33
Rosslare, Co Wexford, 79
Russell, George ('AE'), 32, 82, 93

St Enda's College, Dublin, 93, 94, 95
Saunderson, Edward, 20, 32
Shaw, Bernard, 67
Sion Mills, 75
Somerville, Edith, 3, 86
Swift, Jonathan, ii
Synge, John M., 56, 67

Tempo village, Co Fermanagh, vi
Toome, Co Antrim, 6
Tory Island, 70
Trams, 8
Trinity College, Dublin, 63, 96
tunnel, to Scotland, 12

University of Dublin, viii

Victoria, Queen, vii, 21, 22
Victoria College, Belfast, 91

Walmer Castle, the, vi
Welch, R.J., 57, 80
Westport, Co Mayo, 114
whiskey, 28
White Island, Lower Lough Erne, 66
Whitehead, Co Antrim, 12
Wilberforce, Basil, 110
Wilde, Oscar, 66
Wilson, Stanley, 14
Wolff, G.W., vi

Yeats, W.B., 56, 67, 71, 82
Youghal, Co Cork, iii, 87, 116